Elizabeth Hands

The Death of Amnon

A Poem

Elizabeth Hands

The Death of Amnon
A Poem

ISBN/EAN: 9783744713177

Printed in Europe, USA, Canada, Australia, Japan

Cover: Foto ©Thomas Meinert / pixelio.de

More available books at **www.hansebooks.com**

THE DEATH OF AMNON.

A POEM.

WITH AN

APPENDIX:

CONTAINING

PASTORALS,

AND OTHER

POETICAL PIECES.

By ELIZABETH HANDS.

PRINTED FOR THE AUTHOR,
BY N. ROLLASON, COVENTRY.
M,DCCLXXXIX.

TO

BERTIE GREATHEED, Esq.

SIR,

THE difficulties which an Author, under my circumstances, has to contend with—born in obscurity, and never emerging beyond the lower stations in life—must have been an insurmountable bar to the publication of the following POEMS, had not the approbation and zeal of some particular friends to serve me, been exerted in a manner which demands my most thankful acknowledgments, and with a success which I had little reason to expect. Nothing could have

DEDICATION.

have added more to the satisfaction which I have felt from their flattering efforts, than the permission which I have obtained of prefixing your name to them. This honour from a Gentleman so distinguished for literary, as well as every other polite accomplishment, will, I trust, ensure me the candour, if not the attention of the Public.

I am,

With the greatest respect,

Your most obedient,

And obliged

Humble servant,

ELIZ. HANDS.

LIST OF SUBSCRIBERS.

☞ *Those marked with an Asterisk thus [*] are Subscribers to the Copies printed on fine large Paper.*

A

*AYLESFORD, Right Hon. the Earl of
*Aylesford, Right Hon. the Countess of
*Archer, Right Hon. Lady
*Alston, Sir Rowland, Bart.
*Abington, Mrs.
*Abney, Mrs.
Adams, Simon, Esq.
Adams, Mrs.
Adams, Mr. Poyntz, Daventry
Adams, Mr. Christ College, Cambridge
Adams, Miss, Welton
Adderley, Mrs. Hams-hall
Agutter, Rev. Mr. Magdalen College, Oxon
*Akehurst, Rev. Mr. A.
*Akehurst, Rev. Mr. P.
Allen, Mr. Trinity College, Oxon
Andrews, Charles, Esq.
Andrew, Mr. Queen's College, Cambridge
Ansley, ——, Esq. Bath
Arden, John, Esq.
Ash, John, M. D. London
Askew, Rev. Mr.
Aston, Mr. Thomas, Walworth
Aston, Miss Elizabeth, London
Atkins, Mr. Bourton
Atterbury, Miss, Coventry
Anderson, Mrs.

SUBSCRIBERS.

Awbrey, Mr. Joseph, Lum.
Awson, Abraham, Esq.
Aylworth, Samuel, Esq.
Alexander, Mrs. Norwich

B

*Beaufort, his Grace the Duke of
*Bagot, Right Hon. Lord. *Two copies*
*Bagot, Right Hon. Lady. *Two copies*
Burke, Right Hon. Edmond, M. P.
Barry, Hon. Mr.
Bridgman, Sir Harry, Bart.
*Banks, Sir Joseph, Bart. President R. S.
*Banks, Lady
*Banks, Mrs.
*Banks, Miss
Babington, Mr. St. John's College, Cambridge
Bagshaw, Mr. Bourton
Bailey, Mr. Comb Fields
*Baker, Rev. Mr. Chiddingley
Baldwin, Rev. Mr. Brandon
Baldwin, Mrs.
Banbury, Mr. Princethorpe
Banks, Mr. Trinity Hall, Cambridge
Barnes, Rev. Dr. Vice Chancellor, Cambridge
Barnicle, Mr.
Barnwell, Mr. Bourton
Barnwell, Miss, ditto
Barnwell, Mrs. Charlecote
Barnwell, Mr. John, Draycote
Barnwell, Mr. Richard, ditto
Barnwell, Miss Ann, ditto
Barnwell, Mrs. Hensborough
Barrs, Mr. Thurlaston

SUBSCRIBERS.

Baseley, Mrs. Anne, Wapenbury
Basset, Mr. Barby
Basset, Mr. jun. ditto
Baxter, Dudley, Esq.
Beasley, Mr. Brinklow
Beet, Mrs. Bourton
*Belcher, William, Esq. London
Belcher, Mrs.
Belcher, Miss
Belcher, Miss Lucy
Belcher, Miss Frances
Bell, Mrs. Elizabeth, London
Bennet, Miss, Coventry
Bennet, Mr. Warwick
Bennet, Mrs. ditto
Benson, ——, Esq. Wadham College, Oxon
Benwell, Rev. William, Trinity College, Oxon
Berry, Mr. jun. Bourton
Best, Mr. Magdalen College, Oxon
*Bever, Rev. Mr. Stoke
Beverley, J. Esq. Cambridge
Biddulph, Lieutenant-Colonel John
Biddulph, John, Esq.
Biddulph, William, Esq.
Biker, Rev. Mr. Culworth
Biker, Miss, ditto
Billington, Mrs. Leamington
Billington, Mr. Southam
Birbury, Miss Ann, Stretton
Birch, Mr. Rugby. *Two copies*
Birch, Mr. Warwick
Bird, William Wilberforce, Esq. London
Bird, Mrs. ditto
Bird, William, Esq.
Bird, Miss, Coventry
Bird, Miss M. ditto
Bird, Miss, Coleshill

SUBSCRIBERS.

Bird, Miss Maria, Coleshill
Blencowe, Samuel, Esq.
Blencowe, Mrs.
Blick, Mrs.
Bliss, Rev. Mr. Meriden
Bliss, Mr. Thomas, Hillmorton
Bluett, Mr. Sidney College, Cambridge
Blundel, Mr. Frankton
Blythe, Rev. Mr. Coleshill
Blythe, Rev. Mr. Elmdon
Boddington, Mr. Rugby
Bohun, Mr. Magdalen College, Oxon
Bolding, Mrs. Warwick
Bond, Mrs. Birdingbury
Borsley, Mr. Ladbroke
Borsley, Mrs. Honingham
Borsley, Mrs. Marton
Bosville, Rev. Mr. Magdalen College, Oxon
Bottom, Mr. Dunchurch
Boucher, Rev. Mr.
Boultbee, Joseph, Esq.
Boulton, Mrs. Wellesburne
Bourne, Rev. Dr. Worcester College, Oxon
Bousquet, Mr. Trinity College, Oxon
Bowdler, Mrs. Bath. *Two copies*
Bowen, Mr. Birdingbury
Bower, Rev. Mr. Brazen-Nose College, Oxon
Bowles, Rev. Mr. Lechlade
Bradbury, Miss, Bedworth
Braithwaite, Daniel, Esq.
Brand, T. Esq.
Bree, Rev. Mr. Allesley
Bree, Mrs. ditto
Bree, Rev. Mr. Coleshill
Bree, Mrs. ditto
Bree, Mrs. Stratford-upon-Avon

SUBSCRIBERS.

Brettal, Rev. Mr. Worcester College, Oxon
Bridger, Mr. Magdalen College, Oxon
Brittain, Miss
Broadhead, ——, jun. Esq.
Bromby, Mr. Sidney College, Cambridge
Bromfield, Mr. Trinity College, Oxon
Bromfield, Mrs. Dunchurch
Bromfield, Mr. William, Thurlaston
*Bromley, William Davenport, Esq.
Brooks, Rev. Mr. Coventry
Brothers, Mr. Hungerley
Brothers, Mrs. Ryton
Brown, Mr.
Brown, Mr. Frankton
Browne, Mr.
Browne, Mr. Bartholomew, London
Bruckfield, Mr. T. B. Coventry
Buckland, Rev. Mr. Corpus Christi College, Oxon
Bucknill, Mrs. Rugby
Bucknill, Mrs. S. ditto
Buffery, Mr. Rowington
Bunning, Rev. Mr.
*Burgh, Richard, Esq.
Burrough, Rev. Dr. Magdalen College, Oxon
Burrough, Rev. Mr. Sapcote
Burrows, Miss, Coventry
Bush, Mr. Frankton
Bush, Miss, ditto
Butlin, Mrs. Rugby
Butt, Rev. Mr. Trentham
Bach, Mr. J. Norwich
Barrett, Robert, Esq. Horste
Bell, Mrs. Norwich
Bircham, Mrs. ditto
Bircham, Miss, ditto

SUBSCRIBERS.

Bowyer, Miſs, London
Book Society, Nuneaton

C

*Cremorne, Right Hon. Lord Viſcount. *Two copies*
*Cremorne, Right Hon. Lady Viſcounteſs. *Two copies*
*Conway, Hon. General
Caldecott, Thomas, Eſq. New College, Oxon
Caldecott, Mrs. Warwick
Caldecott, Mr. Samuel, Warwick
Caldecott, Mrs. Rugby
Cantley, Rev. Mr. Molſoe
Cantley, Miſs Lucy, ditto
Capel, Mr. Floore
*Capper, Rev. Mr.
Carpenter, Mr. Henry
Carr, Mr. Coventry
Carter, Mr. John, Willey
Cartwright, Charles, Eſq. London
Caſtel, Mr. Bilton
Cattel, Rev. Mr. Snitterfield
Chambers, Mr. Coventry
Chambers, Rev. Mr. Worceſter College, Oxon
Champagne, Rev. Mr. Nuneaton
*Chaplin, Miſs. *Two copies*
Chapman, Rev. Dr. Preſident of Trinity College, Oxon
Chartres, Rev. Mr. Atherſtone
Chater, Mr. Thomas, Frankton
Chater, Mr. John, ditto
Cheflyn, Mr. Alleſley
*Churton, Rev. Mr. Brazen-Noſe College, Oxon
Clare, Rev. Mr. Atherſtone
Clare, Mr. Claphill
Clare, Mrs. Rugby
Clare, Miſs, ditto
*Clarke, Mrs. Sawbridge
*Clark, Miſs, Welton
*Clark, Miſs M. ditto

*Clay,

SUBSCRIBERS.

*Clay, Thomas, Esq. Coventry
Clay, Mr. St. John's-street, London
Clay, Mrs. Bilton
Cleaver, Mr. Hardwick
Clew, Mr. Upper-Boddington
Cockburn, Mrs. London
Colborne, Mr. Trinity College, Oxon
Cole, Mr. Coventry
Cole, Mr. Stretton
Coleman, Rev. Dr. Master of Bennet College, Cambridge
Coleman, Mrs. Nuneaton
Collett, Mr. University College, Oxon
Collins, Rev. Mr. Claverdon
Collins, Mr. Thomas, Nuneaton
Congreve, Miss, Coventry
Congreve, Miss Ann, ditto
Coomb, Mrs. Bloomsbury-square, London
Coomb, Miss, ditto
Coomb, Mr.
Coney, Mr. Oriel College, Oxon
Conyers, Mrs. Astley
Cooper, Rev. Mr. Loxley
Cooper, Rev. Mr. Yelvertoft
Cooper, Mrs. Harbury
Cormouls, Rev. Mr. Coventry
Cornish, Mr. Charlecote
Corral, Mrs. S. Long-Buckby
Cotterell, Mrs. Bewdley
Cox, Rev. Mr. Leek-Wotton
Cox, Mr. Napton
Cox, Mr. Abraham, Offchurch
*Cox, Mr. Edward, London
*Crachrode, Rev. Mr.
Crew, Miss, Bilton
Cross, Mr. John, London
Crossfield, Miss, Rugby

Crofts,

SUBSCRIBERS.

Crofts, Mr. Mount-Pleasant
Crump, Mr. Coventry
*Currie, Mr.
*Currie, Mr. Isaac
*Currie, Mr. John
*Currie, Mr. Mark
*Currie, Mrs. Mark
*Curson, P. Ashton, Esq.
*Curson, Mrs.
Curtiss, Rev. Mr. Rector, Birmingham
C. Mr. J.
Candler, Mrs. Norfolk

D

*Damer, Hon. Mrs.
*Drake, William, Esq. M. P.
Dadford, Mr. jun.
Dadley, Mr. Edward, London
Dadley, Mr. John Birmingham
Dallaway, Miss S. ditto
Dalton, Mrs. Rugby
Dalton, Mr.
Dalton, Miss
*Daniel, Rev. Mr. Warwick
Daniel, Mrs. Bilton
Daniel, Mrs. S. ditto
Davidson, Rev. Mr. King's College, Cambridge
Davie, Rev. Dr. Trinity College, Oxon
Davie, Rev. C. Sherwell
Davie, Miss, Bristol
Davie, Miss Eustachia, ditto
Davie, Miss Jul. ditto
Davies, Rev. Mr. Newport-Pagnell
*Davis, Rev. Mr. Cranfield
Davis, Mr. Magdalen College, Oxon
Davison, Miss A. Reading
Dawes, Mrs. Warwick
Day, Mr. Magdalen College, Oxon De-Castro,

SUBSCRIBERS.

De-Castro, Mrs. Rugby
*Delabere, Thomas B. Esq.
*Dempster, George, Esq. *Two copies*
Davie, Miss, Southampton
Dewis, Court, Esq. Wellesburne
Dewis, Mr. William, Bedworth
Dickenson, Rev. Mr. Worcester College, Oxon
Dickenson, Mr. Coventry
Dolphin, Miss Mary, Birmingham
Douglass, Mr. William, Coventry
Downing, Mr. Causton
Downing, Mrs. S.
Drace, R. A. Esq. London
Dudley, Rev. Mr. J.
Dudley, Mrs.
Dudley, Mr. John, Coventry
Duffkin, Mrs. Rugby
Dupre, ——, Esq.
Durbin, Rev. Mr. West-Bromwich
*Durnford, Mrs. London
*Dyott, John, Esq.
Dyott, Mr. John Philip
Dyson, Mr. Marton
Dyson, Mrs. ditto
Davison, Mr. John, London. *Two copies.*
Davison, Mr. James, ditto
Decker, Rev. Thomas, Norwich

E

*Edgecumbe, Right Hon. Lord Viscount
*Edgecumbe, Right Hon. Lady Viscountess
*Edgecumbe, Hon. R.
*Edgecumbe, Hon. Lady Sophia
Eagle, Mr. Allesley
Edkins, Mrs. Coleshill
Edwards, Rev. Mr.
Edwards, Mrs.
Eaton, Rev. Dr. Deptford

Elkington,

SUBSCRIBERS.

Elkington, Mr. John
Elkington, Mr. William
Elkington, Miss M.
Elliott, William, Esq.
Elliott, Miss
Ely, Mrs. Newington
*Emans, Rev. Mr. Coventry
England, Miss, ditto
Evans, Mr. sen. Christ College, Cambridge
Evans, Mr. jun. ditto
Ewins, Mr. Great-Houghton
Eyre, Rev. Mr. Solihull

F

Fox, Right Hon. Charles, M. P.
*Fox, Hon. Miss
Fallowfield, Rev. Mr. Daventry
Farborough, Miss, Warwick
*Farmer, Rev. Dr. Master of Emanual College, Cambridge
Farmer, Captain
Farmer, Mr. Berkeswell
Farr, Mr. Coventry
Farrer, Miss, Warmington
Faulkner, Rev. Dr. Lichfield
*Fauquier, Francis, Esq.
*Fauquier, Mrs.
Favre, Mr. London
Fell, Mrs. Rugby
*Fisher, Mr. Magdalen College, Oxon
Fisher, Mr. William, Cambridge
Fitzherbert, Mrs.
Flamank, Rev. Dr. Trinity College, Oxon
Flavel, Mr. Joseph, Thurlaston
*Foley, Mrs.
Folliot, John, Esq. Trinity College, Oxon
Fombelle, Mr. Henry, London
Fombelle, Mr. Peter, ditto
Ford, Mr. Samuel, Birmingham

*Forsteen,

SUBSCRIBERS.

*Forsteen, William, Esq. London
Forster, John, sen. Esq. Leicester-Grange
Forster, John, jun. Esq.
Forster, Mr. St. John's College, Cambridge
Frances, Mrs. Stretton
*Freeman, Thomas, Esq. Daventry
*Frewen, John, Esq. Coldorton
*Frewen, Miss, ditto
Frewen, Miss, Bath
Friend, Mr. William, Dunchurch
Frost, Peter, Esq. London
Frost, Mr. J. Lower-Boddington
Frost, Mr. S. Leamington

G

*Gill, W. Right Hon. Lord Mayor of London
*Gideon, Sir Sampson, Bart. M. P.
*Gideon, S. E. Esq.
*Glynne, Sir Stephen, Bart.
*Glynne, Lady
*Glynne, Francis, Esq.
*Glynne, Miss
Gardner, Rev. Mr. Catherine Hall, Cambridge
Gaskarth, Rev. Mr. Farnborough
Geary, Mrs.
Geary, Rev. Mr. Trinity College, Oxon
Geast, Mr. Richard, Birmingham
Geast, Miss Ann, ditto
Geast, Miss Mary, ditto
Gee, Mr.
Gibbs, Mr. Edmond, Coventry
*Gibbs, Mrs. Ann, Henley
*Gibson, Miss, Pangbourn
Gilby, Dr. Birmingham
Gilkes, Mr. Offchurch
Gilpin, M. Esq.
Godwin, Mrs. Bourton

SUBSCRIBERS.

Gooch, Dr. *Four copies*
Goodall, Mr. S. Briftol
*Goodall, Mifs, Birmingham
Goode, Mr. William, Hardwick
Gordon, Rev. Mr. St. John's College, Cambridge
Gordon, Mifs
Gorton, William, Efq. London
Greatheed, Mr. Newport-Pagnell
Greatheed, Mrs. ditto
*Greenway, Mr. Warwick. *Two copies*
*Greenway, Mrs. ditto
Greatheed, Bertie, Efq. *Seven copies*
Greatheed, Mrs. Marftham. *Seven copies*
Greatheed, Mrs. Warwick
Greatheed, Mifs, ditto
Gregory, Mrs. Stivichall
Gregory, Mifs M. ditto
Gregory, Mifs F. ditto
*Grimes, Abraham, Efq.
Grove, William, Efq.
Grove, Edward, Efq.
Grove, Rev. Thomas, Rotheram
Groves, Mr. T. Daventry
Gunning, Mr. Chrift College, Cambridge
Gilbert, Mifs
Ganning, Mrs. Norwich
Gay, Mrs. ditto

H

*Hautford, Marquis de
Hewitt, Hon. William
Hill, Hon. Mr.
Hatton, Lady
*Hacket, Andrew, Efq.
*Hacket, Mrs.
Hakefley, Mr. Edward, jun. Branfton
Hakefley, Mr. Thomas, ditto
Hall, Mr.   Halford,

SUBSCRIBERS.

Halford, ——, Esq.
Hall, Mr.
*Halstead, Thomas, Esq.
Halstead, Rev. Mr. Tamworth
Hanbury, Mr. Westminster
Hancox, Mr. Thomas, Ryton
*Hands, George, Esq. Lichfield
Hands, Mrs. Susannah, Napton
Hands, Mr. Josiah, Stoneley
Harding, Miss
Hardwick, Mrs.
Hardy, Mrs. Isabella, London
Harriott, Rev. Mr. Elmdon
Harris, Mr.
Harris, Mr. Milk-street, London
Harris, Mr. H. Offchurch
*Harris, Mrs. Honingham
Harris, Mrs. Rugby
Harris, Mrs. S. ditto
Harris, Mrs. Twyford
Harrison, Henry B. Esq. Daventry
Harrison, Rev. Mr. Magdalen College, Oxon
Harrison, Mr. W. B. Merton College, Oxon
Harrison, Miss, Wolverton
Harrold, Miss, Temple-Balsall
Hartlett, Miss, Coventry
Hartley, Rev. Mr. Christ College, Cambridge
*Hartopp, Edward Cradock, Esq.
Hassal, Mrs. Solyhull
Hassal, Miss Mary, Rugby
Hawkes, Mr. Thomas, Henley
Hawkes, Miss, Charlecote
Hayward, Mrs. Harrietsham
*Heber, Rev. Mr. Malpas
Hedges, Mr. Henry, London
Hemming, Mr. S.

Herbert,

SUBSCRIBERS.

Herbert, Mr. T. Rowington
Herbert, Mrs.
Hewitt, Mrs. R. Draycote
Hewitt, Mr. S. Stretton
Heydon, Mr. John, Banbury
*Heydon, Mr. Richard, ditto
Heygate, Mr. J. London
Heyrick, Mr. William, Leicester
Higgins, Mr. John, Weston
Higgins, Miss, ditto
*Higgenson, Mr. London. *Two copies*
Higham, Mr. William, Pattishall
Highmore, Rev. Samuel, King's College, Cambridge
Hill, Mr. J. Rugby
Hill, Mr. T. Thurlaston
Hind, Rev. Mr. Magdalen College, Oxon
Hincks, Mr. Eathorpe
Hincks, Mrs. Martha, Daventry
Hiorn, Mr. Warwick
Hirons, Mr. Wolston
Hoare, Rev. Dr. Principal of Jesus College, Oxon
Hobday, Mr. J. Stretton
Hodges, J. H. Esq.
Hodges, Mr. Emanual College, Cambridge
Hodgett, Miss
Hodgkinson, Rev. Mr. Reading
Holbech, William, Esq.
*Holden, Rev. Mr. Queen-street, Westminster
Holden, Mr. B. Wolston
*Holled, Rev. Dr. Barby
Hollingsworth, Mrs. Newport-Pagnell
Hollis, Mr. John, Stretton
Homer, Rev. Henry, sen.
*Homer, Rev. Henry, jun.
Homer, Mr. Edward, Birmingham
Homer, Mr. Edward, London
Homer, Rev. Arthur, Magdalen College, Oxon   Homer,

SUBSCRIBERS.

Homer, Rev. Philip B. Rugby. *Two copies*
*Homer, Mr. Richard, London
Homer, Mr. Thomas, Coventry
Homer, Mr. Charles, Nottingham
Homer, Mr. William, Chriſt College, Cambridge
Homer, Miſs
Homer, Miſs D.
Hooton, Miſs S. Newport-Abbey
Hopkins, Mrs. Warwick
Hopkinſon, Rev. Mr.
Hopkinſon, Mr. Magdalen College, Oxon. *Two copies*
Horbery, Mrs. Lichfield
*Horne, Rev. Dr. Dean of Canterbury
Horne, Mrs. Frankton
*Horſley, Miſs
Herwood, Mr. Trentham
Hoſkins, Rev. Mr. Magdalen College, Oxon
Howkins, Captain, Rugby
Howlett, Mr. Thomas, Rowington
*Huddesford, Rev. John
*Huddesford, Rev. George
Huddesford, Miſs, Alleſley. *Two copies*
Huddesford, Miſs Rebecca, ditto
Huddesford, Miſs Elizabeth, ditto. *Two copies*
Huddesford, Mr. ditto
Huddesford, Mrs. Oxon
Hughes, Rev. Mr. Skennington
Hughes, Rev. Mr. Worceſter College, Oxon.
Hughes, Mr. Welleſburne
Huilh, Mr. Nottingham
Hume, Miſs, Rugby
Hunt, Rev. Mr. King's College, Cambridge
*Hunt, Mr.
*Hunter, Mrs.
Hurlock, Mr. Philip, London
*Hurſt, Rev. Mr. Magdalen College, Oxon

SUBSCRIBERS.

Hurſt, Rev. Mr. Worceſter College, Oxon
Huſbands, Mr. Coventry
Hutchins, Mrs. Anſley
Hyde, Mr. James, London

I

*Johnſton, Right Hon. Lady Cecilia
*Johnſton, General
Jackſon, John, Eſq.
Jackſon, Mr. William, Granborough
Jackſon, Miſs, Bedworth
James, Rev. Dr. Rugby
James, Mrs.
James, Mr. John, Cambridge
Jaques, Rev. Mr. Packington
Ibbetſon, Mr. Richard, Spa-houſe
Jeacock, Mr. Biſhop's-Itchington
Jeacock, Mr. Bubbenhall
Jemſon, Mr. S. Daventry
Jenner, Rev. Mr. Worceſter College, Oxon
Jennet, Miſs, Coventry
Jephcote, Mr. Richard, Willoughby
*Jervoiſe, J. C. jun. Eſq. M. P.
Jeſſe, Rev. J. Compton
Ilett, Miſs, Kineton
Iliffe, Mr. Hillmorton
Inde, Mr. Cambridge
*Inge, Rev. Mr. Lichfield
*Inge, Rev. Mr. Rugeley
Inge, Rev. Mr. Chriſt College, Oxon
*Inge, Miſs, Lichfield
Inge, Mrs. Coventry
Innis, Rev. Mr. Rugby
Innis, Mrs.
Johnſon, Rev. N. P. Emanual College, Cambridge
Johnſon, Thomas, Eſq. Leeds
Johnſon, Mrs. Rebecca, Dunchurch
Johnſon, Mrs. Elizabeth, ditto

Jones,

SUBSCRIBERS.

Jones, Mr. St. John's College, Cambridge
Jordan, Mr. John, London
Isaacson, Mr. Christ College, Cambridge
Judd, Mr. William, Stretton

K

Keen, Mr. Thomas, Stretton
Kellam, Mr. Edward, Ryton
Kelly, Miss, Bedworth
Kening, Rev. Mr. Rugby
Kenwrick, Rev. Dr. Atherstone
Kett, Rev. Mr. Trinity College, Oxon
Key, Rev. Mr.
Kimbell, Mrs. Dean-street, London
Kinderley, John, Esq. London
Kipling, Rev. Mr.
Knibb, Mr. Charlcote
Knight, Mrs. Rugby
Knight, Mrs. Ann, Stretton
Knighton, Lieutenant
*Knightley, John, Esq.
Knightley, Mrs.
Knightley, Rev. Mr. Byfield
Knightley, Rev. Mr. Charlton
Knipe, Mr. Queen's College, Oxon

L

*Lansdown, Right Hon. Marquis of. *Two copies*
*Landaff, Right Rev. Lord Bishop of
Lichfield and Coventry, Right Rev. Lord Bishop of
*Legge, Hon. Mr. Edward, Christ College, Oxon
*Legge, Hon. Augustus
*Legge, Heneage, Esq.
*Legge, Mrs.
*Ladbroke, Robert, Esq. M. P.
Ladbroke, Mr. John, Rugby
Lander, Mr. Wishaw
Landon, Rev. Mr. Worcester College, Oxon
Lant, Mr. Allesley

Lane,

SUBSCRIBERS.

Lane, Rev. Mr. Christ College, Cambridge
Langham, Mr. John, Sidney College, ditto
La Roque, Rev. Mr. Priors-Hardwick
Latimer, Mrs. Marton
Lawley, William, Esq. Bath
Lawrence, Mrs. Leamington-Priors
Lawrence, Mrs. Wapenbury
Lea, Mr. Coventry
Leake, Dr. London
Lee, Mr. David, Coventry
Leggate, Mr. Henley
Levett, Mr. Christ College, Oxon
*Lewis, H. Grefwold, Esq.
Lewis, Mrs. Coventry
Lightoler, Miss, Warwick
Lilly, Mr. Charles, Coventry
Line, Mr. Robert, Long-Lawford
Linnel, Mr. John, Harberbury
Little, Thomas, Esq.
Little, William, Esq.
Loader, Mr. William, London
Loins, Mr. H. Birdingbury
Lombe, Mr. Cambridge. *Two copies*
Long, Robert, Esq.
Long, William, Esq.
*Loveday, Dr.
*Loveday, Mrs.
*Loveday, Mr. Magdalen College, Oxon
*Loveday, Miss
*Loveday, Mr. William, jun. London
Loveday, Mrs. ditto
*Lomb, Sir John, Bart. Norfolk
Lickorish, Rev. R.
*Lowe, Jeremiah, Esq.
Lowe, Mr. Oriel College, Oxon
Lowke, Mr. Willoughby
Lowth, Rev. Mr. Prebendary

Lucas,

SUBSCRIBERS.

*Lucas, William, Esq.
Lucy, Miss, Charlcote
*Ludford, John, Esq.
*Ludford, Mrs.
Ludford, Miss, Camp-Hill
Ludford, Miss Frances
Ludford, Miss Millicent
Luke, Mr. Robert, Sidney College, Cambridge
Lutterworth Society
Lyon, Miss Sarah, London

M.

Mansfield, Right Hon. the Earl of
Middleton, Right Hon. Lady
Murray, Hon. Miss
Murray, Hon. Miss
*Mordaunt, Sir John, Bart.
*Mordaunt, Lady
*Mordaunt, Mrs. Warwick
*Mordaunt, Miss
*Mordaunt, Miss Sophia
Marsh, Miss, Norwich
Mann, Mr. Edward, Wolston
Mackorkel, Mr. Birmingham
*Madan, Rev. Mr. Rector, ditto
Malin, Miss, Rugby
Mallory, Robert, Esq.
*Malony, Mr. Arthur
Mander, Miss, Coventry. *Two copies*
Mann, Mr. C. Stretton
*Mansfield, James, Esq. King's Counsel
Manton, Mrs. H.
Manwaring, Mr. St. John's College, Cambridge
Mapletoft, Rev. Edmund
Mapletoft, Mr. Emanual College, Cambridge
Marriott, Rev. Dr. Cottesbatch
Mariss, Mr. Exeter College, Cambridge
Markam, Mr. Thomas, Napton

Marshall,

SUBSCRIBERS.

Marshall, Miss, Meriden
Marsam, Mr. Thomas
Martin, Mr. St. John's College, Cambridge
Martin, Mr. John, Dunchurch
Martin, Mrs. Bayswater
*Martin, Mrs. White-Knights
Mason, Thomas, Esq. Temple
Mason, Mr. Wallis, Birmingham
Mason, Mrs. M. Stretton
Massingberd, Rev. Mr. Magdalen College, Oxon. *Two copies*
Masters, Mr. R. Birdingbury
Masters, Mr. T. Stretton
Masters, Mrs. S. Birdingbury
Masters, Mrs. Long-Lawford
Masters, Mrs. Wellesburne
Matthews, Rev. Mr. Magdalen College, Oxon
Matthews, Mr. Pembroke Hall, Cambridge
Maule, Rev. Mr. King's College, Cambridge
Mauleverer, ——, Esq. London
Maynard, Anthony Lax, Esq.
Mayo, Mr. St. John's College, Oxon
Mayo, Mrs. Stratford
Meachers, Mrs. Newport-Pagnell
Mead, Rev. Mr. Magdalen College, Oxon
*Medcalf, Major
Mence, Mr. J. Worcester College, Oxon
Merridew, Mrs. Coventry
Methold, Rev. Mr. Trinity College, Oxon
Mieres, Mrs. Lichfield
Millar, A. Grammar, Esq.
*Millar, Fiennes, Esq.
*Mills, Rev. Mr. Barford
Mills, Mrs. ditto
Millington, Mr. Rugby
Minster, Mr. William, Coventry
Mompesson, Mrs. Mansfield-Woodhouse
Monckton, Mr.

Moor,

SUBSCRIBERS.

Moor, Mr. J. Sidney College, Cambridge
Moor, Mrs. Rugby
Moor, Miss, Charlecote
Morice, Mr. John, London. *Two copies*
Morse, Rev. Mr. Marton
Moul, Mrs. Hagley-Row
Moulding, Rev. Mr. Trinity College, Oxon
Mowe, Mrs. Wolston. *Two copies*
Muckleston, Rev. Mr. Lichfield
Munday, Millar, Esq.
Murcott, Mr. Francis
*Murcott, Mrs. Cubbington
Murcott, Miss H. Bubbenhall
Murthwaite, Rev. Mr. Brackley
Musson, Mr. Rugby
*Musson, Miss, Baginton
Mitchell, Mr. Cambridge

N

Newdigate, Sir Roger, Bart.
Newdigate, Lady
*Northcote, Sir Stafford, Bart.
Nairne, Rev. Mr. Lillington
Nall, Mrs. Ann, Warwick
Neal, Mr. William, Rowington
Neale, Mr. J. M. London
Neale, Mrs. Allesley
Neale, Mrs. Frankton
Newberry, Francis, Esq.
Newcomb, Mr. John, Southam
Newcomb, Mr. William, ditto
Newcomb, Miss, ditto
Newsham, Mrs. Harborough-Magna
*Newton, Mrs. Coventry
*Nicholls, Mr.
*Nicholls, Mr. Queen-street, London
*Nichols, Mrs. Whitchurch
*Norris, James, Esq. Norwich. *Two copies*

SUBSCRIBERS.

Norris, Mr. Caius College, Cambridge
Norris, Mr. Chrift College, Cambridge
Norris, Mr. Thomas, Bubbenhall
Norris, Mr. William, Marton
Nutcombe, Mr. Sidney College, Cambridge
Nutt, Mrs.

O

Oakes, Charles, Efq.
Okeover, Rowland, Efq.
Olormfhaw, Mr. Richard
Only, Rev. Mr. Newbold
Ord, Mr. Chrift Church College, Oxon
Orton, Mr. John, Bubbenhall
Orton, Mrs. Rugby
Over, Mr. Hardwick
Owen, Mr. jun. Coventry
Okes, Mr. Cambridge

P

Pufey, Hon. ———
Page, Mifs, Eydon
Pagett, Mr. J. Bourton
Palfrey, Mr. E. J. Coventry
Palmer, Edward, Efq. Birmingham
Palmer, Rev. Edward, Colefhill
Palmer, Mr. Kimbolton
Palmer, Mrs. Ladbroke
Parker, George, Efq. St. John's College, Cambridge
Parker, Rev. Mr. Newbold
Parker, Mr. Abraham, Farnborough
Parker, Mrs. Lichfield
Parkhurft, Fl. Efq.
*Parkinfon, Rev. Mr. Chrift College, Cambridge
Parr, Rev. Dr. *Two copies*
Parr, Rev. Mr.
Parrott, Mr. Frankton
Parry, Mr. Warwick
Parry, Mrs.
Parfons, Rev. Mr. Leeds

Parfons,

SUBSCRIBERS.

Parsons, Mr. Thomas, Long-Lawford
Paterson, Mr. George, London
Paterson, Miss, ditto
Payne, Mr. Bookseller, London. *Six copies*
Payne, Mr. William, Coventry
Pearson and Rollason, Birmingham
Peat, Mr. A. London
Peele, Mrs. Norwich
Penson, Mr. Thomas, Oxon
Pepperill, Rev. Mr.
Pepperill, Miss
Percival, Mr. John, Northampton
Perkins, Mr. Thomas, Coventry. *Two copies*
Perkins, Mrs. Pattishall
Phillips, Mr. William, Offchurch
Pickering, Rev. Mr. Winson-Green
Pickering, Mr. Rugby
Piercy, Mr. Robert, Bedworth
Piggot, Mr. T. Dunchurch
Piggot, Miss
Pilliner, Mr. London
Pitt, Mr. Shoe-lane, ditto
Plomer, Miss, Welton
Pollard, Mr.
Porteous, Mr. Holborn, London
Porter, Rev. Mr. Christ College, Cambridge
Powel, Mrs. Rugby
Price, Rev. Mr. Badl. Librarian, Oxon
Price, Mr. Isaac, Coventry
*Prinsep, John, Esq. Pall-Mall
*Prinsep, Mrs.
Proby, Mr. St. John's College, Cambridge
Prosser, Rev. Mr. Baliol College, Oxon
Pye, Mr. Merton College, Oxon

Q

Quinney, Mr. Marton

R

Rainbow, Mrs. Branston

SUBSCRIBERS.

Rann, Rev. Mr. Coventry
Rann, Mr. Joseph, ditto
Rattray, Dr. ditto
Reader, William, Esq. ditto
Reading, Mrs. Leamington
Reay, H. U. Esq.
Redfern, Mr. Joseph, Birmingham
Reed, Isaac, Esq. London
Remington, Miss, Stretton
Renny, Miss, Newport-Pagnell
Repton, Book-Club Society
Reynolds, Rev. Mr. King's College, Cambridge
Rice, Mr. Tamworth
Rich, Miss, Sunning
Richards, Mr. Bubbenhall
Richards, Mrs. Birmingham
*Richardson, William, Esq. London
Richardson, Mrs. Daventry
Riland, Rev. Mr. Sutton-Coldfield
Riland, Mrs.
Roadnight, Mr. Dunchurch
Roadnight, Mr. Marton
Roberts, Mr. jun. Cavendish-square, London
Roberts, Mr. Wincobank
Roberts, Mr. T. Honingham
Robinson, Rev. Mr. Christ Church College, Oxon
Robinson, Rev. Mr. Christ College, Cambridge
Robinson, Mr. Magdalen College, Oxon. *Two copies*
Rodwell, Mr. Thomas
Rogers, Mr.
*Rogers, Mrs.
Rollason, Mr. Coventry. *Three copies*
Rollins, Mr. B. Towcester
*Rose, Rev. Mr. Daventry
Routh, Rev. Mr. Magdalen College, Oxon. *Two copies*
Rowel, Mrs. Rugby
Robinson, Mr. Cambridge
*Rugby, Book-Club Society   Rushworth,

SUBSCRIBERS.

Rushworth, Mrs. Banbury
Russell, Mr. William, Dunchurch
Russell, Miss, ditto
Russell, Mrs. Kenilworth
Ruston, Mrs. Deritend, Birmingham
*Ryder, Mrs. Lichfield

S

Sandwich, Right Hon. Earl of
*Sheffield, Right Hon. Lord
Stormont, Right Hon. Lord
*Shuckburgh, Sir George A. Bart. M. P.
*Shuckburgh, Lady. *Two copies*
Skipwith, Lady. *Seven copies*
Sadler, Millar, Esq.
Sadler, Rev. Mr. Coleshill
Salmon, Mr. George, Causton
Salmon, Mr. Robert, Weekly
Sammelles, Mr.
Sanders, Thomas, Esq.
Sandys, Rev. Mr. Eversholt
Saul, Mr. William, Byfield
Sawbridge, Mr. Alderman, London
*Schomberg, Rev. Mr. Magdalen College, Oxon
*Scott, Mrs. Wolston. *Two copies*
Scullard, William, Esq.
Seagrave, Mr. Worcester College, Oxon
*Seale, Rev. Dr. Lambeth
Secker, ——, Esq. Windsor
Seward, Miss, Lichfield
Shettle, Mr. C. Stretton
Shettle, Mrs. ditto
*Sharman, Mr. Thomas, Wolston
Sharp, Richard, Esq.
Sharp, Mr. Warwick
*Shaw, Rev. Mr.
Scott, Mr. Cambridge
Shaw, Rev. Mr. All Souls College, Oxon

SUBSCRIBERS.

Shaw, Rev. Mr. Magdalen College, Oxon
Sheasby, Mr. Tamworth
Short, Mr. Trinity College, Oxon
Shuckburgh, John, Esq. *Four copies*
Shuckburgh, Rev. Mr. Bourton
Shuckburgh, Mrs. *Three copies*
Simons, Mrs. Coventry
Simpson, Robert, Esq. ditto
Simpson, Charles, Esq. Lichfield
Simpson, Mrs. ditto
*Sisson, Rev. Mr. Christ Church College, Oxon
Sitwell, ———, Esq.
Sitwell, Mrs. Stainsby
*Skinner, Rev. Mr.
Sleath, Rev. Mr. Rugby
Sleath, Mr. John, ditto
Sleath, Miss, Calverton
*Smith, Rev. Mr. Hulcot
Smith, Mr. Christ College, Cambridge
Smith, Mr. C. Rugby. *Two copies*
Smith, Mr. Lilly, Kenilworth
Smith, Mr. Thomas, Langley
Smith, Mrs. Coventry
Smith, Mrs. Bilton
Smith, Miss, Stamford
Snape, Mr. Wishaw
Snow, Mr. Southam
Snow, Mr. Offchurch
Soden, Mr. Jonathan, Comb-Fields
Soden, Mr. Frankton
Soden, Miss, Rowington
Southgate, Rev. Mr.
Spooner, ———, Esq. Elmdon
*Spooner, Mrs. ditto
Spooner, Mr. Abraham
Spooner, Mr. Isaac
Spooner, Mr. T. Dunchurch
Stafford, Rev. Egerton   Stanfield

SUBSCRIBERS.

Stanfield, Mr. John
Stanley, Mrs. P. Egham
Stanton, John, Esq.
Stanton, William, Esq.
Steane, Mr. Edward, Leamington
Steane, Mrs. Coventry
*Steevens, George, Esq.
Stephens, Henry, Esq. Trinity College, Oxon
Stevenson, ——, Esq.
Stevens, Rev. Mr. Repton
Stevens, Mr. William, Sidney College, Cambridge
Steward, Miss, Kenilworth
Steward, Miss, Winson-Green
Stillingfleet, Mr. Christ Church College, Oxon
Stodart, Miss, Rugby
Storer, Rev. Dr. Canterbury
Stretton, Miss
Stubbin, Mr. Trinity College, Oxon
Suckling, Mr. Trinity College, Oxon
Suffield, Thomas, Esq. Norwich
Summer, Rev. Mr. Stareton
Sutton, Mrs. Offchurch
Sutton, Miss, Dunchurch
Sylvester, Mr. John, Thurlaston
*Symonds, Rev. Mr. Cambden

T

Taylor, Mr. J. Birmingham
Taylor, Rev. Mr. Trinity College, Oxon
Taylor, Mr. Jonathan, Coventry
Taylor, Mrs. Highgate
Tebbitts, Mr. Robert, Long-Itchington
Tennant, Mr.
Thackeray, Mrs. Cambridge
*Tibbits, Richard, Esq.
Todd, Mrs. Newington
Tomlinson, Mr. Birmingham
Toms, Rev. Mr. Coventry
*Tibbits, Mrs.

Townsend,

SUBSCRIBERS.

Townsend, Gore, Esq.
Townsend, Mr. Long-Lawford
Townsend, Miss, Bourton
Townsend, Miss J. ditto
*Townson, Rev. Dr. Malpas
*Townson, John, Esq. London
Troth, Mr. Rowington
Trotman, Mrs. Harberbury
*Troughton, Bryan, Esq.
Troughton, Mr. James, Coventry
Truslove, Mr. Bourton
Truslove, Mrs. Potford-Dam
Truslove, Miss, Hill
Truswell, Mr. Thomas, Nuneaton
Tupen, Mr. William, Brighthelmstone
Turnbull, Dr.
Turner, Mr. John, Flecknoe
Turner, Mr. John, Honingham
Turner, Mrs. Rugby
Twigger, Mr. Job
Tyson, Richard, Esq. M. C. Bath

U

Umbers, Mr. Weston
Underwood, Miss, London
Uthwatt, Mrs. Lindford

V

Valentine, Mr. John, Leicester
*Vatas, Rev. Mr. Caversham
Vaughan, Benjamin, Esq. London
Vaughan, Mr. P. Merton College, Oxon
Vaughan, Rev. Mr. Trinity College, Oxon
Veasy, Mr. William, Wolston
Venning, Mr. Milk-street, London
Venour, John, Esq. Worcester College, Oxon
Ventriss, Rev. Mr. Magdalen College, Oxon
Vernon, Mr. Coventry
*Vernon, Miss, ditto
*Villers, Mr. ditto

Villers,

SUBSCRIBERS.

Villers, Mr. John, ditto
Villers, Miss, ditto
Villers, Mr. William, Birmingham
*Vincent, Mrs. Worcester
*Vyner, Rev. Dr.
Vyner, Mr. Robert
Vyner, Mrs. Eathorpe
Vyner, Mrs. Rugby

W

*Warwick, Right Hon. Earl of. *Two copies*
*Warwick, Right Hon. Countess of. *Two copies*
Worcester, Right Hon. Marquis of
*Wycombe, Right Hon. Earl of. *Two copies*
Windham, W. Right Hon. M. P.
*Woodhouse, Sir John, Bart. M. P.
*Woodhouse, Lady
Wheler, Sir William, Bart.
Wheler, Lady
Wace, Mr. London
Wait, Mr. William, Branston
Walford, Mr. Birmingham
Walker, J. Esq. London
Walker, Thomas, Esq. ditto
Walker, Rev. Mr. Mears-Ashby
Walker, Mrs. Newbold
*Wall, Dr. Clin. Lect. Oxon. *Two copies*
*Wall, Mrs.
Wall, Mr. Richard, London
Wall, Mrs. Coventry
Walshman, Mr. Newington
Ward, Mr. Henley
Ward, Mr. Philip, Linford
Warner, Mr. Queen's College, Oxon
Warner, Mrs. Warwick
Warre, Rev. Mr. Rugby
Warren, Mr. John, Prior's-Hardwick
Warren, Mr. H. Frankton
Warton, Rev. Thomas, Poet Laureat, Oxon

Watkins,

SUBSCRIBERS.

Watkins, Mrs. jun. Daventry
Watson, Rev. Mr. Stretton
Watson, Mr. Eathorpe
Watson, Mr. Harborough
Watts, Mr. Binley
Watts, Mrs.
Wear, Rev. Mr. Rowington
Webb, Mr.
Webb, Mr. John, Bourton
Webb, Mr. John, jun. ditto
Webb, Mrs. Henry, ditto
Webb, Mr. John, Claverdon
Webb, Mr. Richard, Granborough
Webb, Mr. Richard, Long-Lawford
Webb, Mr. Henry, Hill
Webb, Miss, Sherburn
Wedge, Mr. Packington
*Welford, John, Esq. London
Wells, Rev. Mr. Worcester College, Oxon
Wells, Miss, Stratford
Welton, Mr. Richard, Marton
Welton, Mrs. ditto
*West, Mrs. Alscott. *Four copies*
West, Miss, ditto
West, Mr. Joseph, Coventry
West, Mr. Snitterfield
West, Mrs. ditto
Weston, James, Esq.
Weston, Mr. Solihull
Weston, Mr. Brixworth
Weston, Mrs. Warwick
Wetherell, Rev. Dean. *Four copies*
*Whateley, ——, Esq.
Wheler, Knightley, Esq.
*Wheler, Trevor, Esq.
Wheler, Francis, Esq.
*Wheler, Rev. Mr. John. *Four copies*
Wheler, Mr. Charles, jun. London

Wheler,

SUBSCRIBERS.

Wheler, Mr. William, Trinity College, Oxon
*Wheler, Mrs. Edward. *Four copies*
Wheler, Mrs. Charles, Leamington
Wheler, Miss, ditto
White, Dr. Professor, Oxon
Whitehead, Mr. T. Offchurch
Whitehead, Mr. G. Ryton
Whitehead, Mrs. A. Birdingbury
Whitehead, Mrs. M. ditto
Whitfield, John, Esq. London
Whitman, Mr. Joseph, Wolston
Whitman, Mr. William, ditto
*Whitwell, Mr. Coventry. *Two copies*
Wilcox, Mr.
Willard, Mr. Thomas, Brighthelmstone
Williams, Rev. Mr. Napton
Williams, Rev. Mr. Wellesburne
Williams, Mr. Bradwell
Williams, Mrs. ditto
Williams, Mr. Edward, London
Williams, Mrs. Alscott
Williams, Mrs. Rugby
Williams, Mrs. London
Williamson, Rev. Mr. Winwick
Williamson, Mr. R. Daventry
Willington, Mr. William, Tamworth
Willis, Mr. Heits
Willis, ——, Esq.
*Wilmer, Mr. Coventry
*Wilmer, Mrs.
*Wilmot, John, Esq. M. P.
*Wilmot, Mr. Edward, Cambridge
Wilmot, Mrs. Derby
Winter, Mrs.
Wise, Matthew, jun. Esq.
*Wise, Mrs. Warwick
Willet, Robert, Esq. London
Wood, Mr. sen. Coventry

Wood,

SUBSCRIBERS.

Wood, Mr. William, Coventry
Woodcock, Mr. Trinity College, Oxon
Wooderfield, Mrs. Highgate
Woodeſon, Dr. Vin. Prof. Oxon
Woodfield, Mrs. Banbury
Woodhouſe, Mrs. Bath
Woodhouſe, Miſs, Bedworth
Woodruff, Mr. Thomas, London
Woodrouffe, Mr. Coventry
Woolley, Mr. Birmingham
Worral, Mr. Thomas, Leamington-Priors
Worth, Mr. John, Dunchurch
Wratiſlavia, Mrs. Rugby
*Wright, William, Eſq. London
Wright, Rev. Mr. Emanual College, Cambridge
Wright, Mr. London
Wright, Sir Sampſon, Knt. Alderman of London
Wright, Mrs. Southam

Y

*Yardley, Mrs. Coventry
Yates, Rev. Mr.
Yates, Mrs. Solihull
Yeoman, Mr. Worceſter College, Oxon
Young, Mr. Richard, Whitnaſh
Young, Miſs, Ardley

Z

Zinzan, Mrs. Reading. *Two copies*

SUBSCRIBERS,
Whoſe Names came too late to be Inſerted in their proper Places.

Beales, Mr. Cambridge
Bullen, Mr. ditto
Burleigh, Mr. ditto
Hodſon, Mr. ditto
Hopkins, Mr. ditto
Hume, Mrs. Knightſbridge.

CONTENTS.

☞ *Those marked thus [*] were, a few years since, inserted in the* Coventry Mercury.

                                                                   Page.

AMNON, Death of	Canto I.	1
	——— II.	12
	——— III.	18
	——— IV.	29
	——— V.	36
On the Supposition of an Advertisement in a Morning Paper, of the Publication of a Volume of Poems by a Servant Maid		47
On the Supposition of the Book having been published and read		50
*Wit and Beauty. A Pastoral		56
*Absence and Death. A Pastoral		59
*Damon, Laura, and Daphne. A Pastoral		62
Love and Friendship. A Pastoral		66
Corydon and Pastora. A Pastoral		69
*Thirsis and Daphne. A Pastoral		72
Observation thereon		73
Damon and Theron. A Pastoral Dialogue		74
Thirsis and Daphne. A Poem		76
Perplexity. A Poem		78
A Pastoral Song		80
The Favourite Swain		82
On a Wedding		85
Lob's Courtship		86
The Rural Maid in London, to her Friend in the Country. An Epistle		88
Corinna to Lycidas		90
An Epistle. Belinda to Maria		91

Leander

CONTENTS.

	Page.
Leander and Belinda. A Tale	93
Observation on an Evening, and Reflection	96
Written while the Author sat on a Cock of Hay	97
On Contemplative Ease	100
Written on their Majesties going to Kew	101
Contentment	103
The Widower's Courtship	104
Observation on the Works of Nature	106
An Elegy	107
Friendship. An Ode	109
Phillis to Damon. A Song	111
On an Unsociable Family	113
Reflection on Meditation	113
On reading Pope's Eloiza to Abelard	114
Written, originally extempore, on seeing a Mad Heifer run through the Village where the Author lives	115
A Song	117
A Song	118
A Song	119
Absence	120
To Thirsis, on his signifying his intention to lay aside his Hautboy	122
On the Author's Lying-In	123
An Enigma	125
Critical Fragments on some of the English Poets	126

THE

DEATH OF AMNON.

A POEM.

THE
DEATH OF AMNON.

CANTO THE FIRST.

THE Royal youth I sing, whose sister's charms
Inspir'd his heart with love; a latent love
That prey'd upon his health; he droop'd; so droops
A beauteous flow'r, when in the stalk some vile
Opprobrious insect 'bides. In conscious pain
He pass'd the hapless hours, while in his breast
Th' aspiring passion, yet by virtue sway'd,
It's proper limits knew. I love, said he,
Whom do I love? my sister—ah; my sister;
Can I my misplac'd passion gratify,
And bring disgrace on her? No, sweetest maid,
I am thy brother; 'tis a brother's part
Thy honour to protect and not destroy.
When Shechem burning with untam'd desire

Dishonour'd Dinah, how her brethren rag'd!
Each took his sword, the princely ravisher,
And every citizen a victim fell
To their just fury.   I'm an Isra'lite;
Shall I forego this high prerogative,—
And plunge myself and sister into ruin?
An act that ev'n an heathen would degrade.
No; sooner shall my passion unreveal'd
Lie cank'ring in my bosom, till it taints
My very blood, and stops my panting breath.
Better my lov'd companions pass my grave,
And shed a tear to think I died so young,
Than shun me living as a vile reproach
To nature, royalty, and Israel.
Already I perceive my strength to fail,
The ruddy bloom of health forsakes my cheeks;
Perhaps death's not far off.—O welcome guest,
Hasten thy tardy steps, why linger'st thou,
Or wait'st on those, who wish thee far away?
O thou, that hast the pow'rs of life and death,
Take hence my life, and end my wretchedness.
A spacious land I see on ev'ry side
Bless'd with fertility; the cultur'd vales
Yield plenteous crops; the rising hills are rich,
With verdant pasture mantled, crown'd with trees;

My

My father's kingdom this.—What is't to me?
It fires not my ambition, all I afk
Is one fmall fpot of earth to lay me down
Beneath the turf, forgetting and forgot,
A fmall requeft, and yet though fmall, denied.
Methinks I feel my ftrength renew'd; 'tis fo;
Struggling with life I figh for death in vain.
Again my paffions rife, again rebel;
I ftill muft live and live in mifery.
But I've a thought, that ftings me yet more deep;
Doubtlefs fome happy rival will be crown'd
With Tamar's love; O tort'ring thought, muft I
Behold her deck'd in bridal robes to blefs
A rival; 'tis too much;—I cannot bear
E'en to fuppofe it, I'll from court retire;
My gay companions now are irkfome grown,
And all my pleafures are transform'd to pains.
My fifter's cheering fmiles, that once convey'd
Soft raptures to my heart, awake fuch pangs,
As I can fcarce endure. Again I feel
My fpirits fink; Oh! welcome fading ficknefs!
I'll cherifh thee and aid thee with my fighs,
To ftill this heart, that now rebellious beats
Againft my reafon's ftrongeft argument.
Though Tamar's beauty prompts my warmeft wifh,

Her fairer virtues keep me still in awe,
Forbidding my aspir'ing love to soar.
With sweet simplicity she smiles, secure
In innocence, commanding my respect,
And this command I must—I will obey;
But fly her presence, lest some hapless smile
Inflame my soul, and I in passions phrensy
Should act against my final resolution
To bear my griefs untold, and secret pine
Till sadd'ning sorrow sinks me to the grave.
Thus, to himself complaining, he resolv'd,
Nor sought a confidant to share his grief.
A friend he had, the son of Shimlah,
Nam'd Jonadab; a man by nature subtle,
Proud and ambitious; yet would meanly stoop
To the most base and most ignoble acts,
To serve his private ends. The artless youth
Oft to its plausibilities gave ear,
Not e'en suspecting, that beneath the cloak
Of formal flatt'ries self-int'rest hides
It's serpent head. Yet still the youth from him
His wayward passion labour'd to conceal,
By forcing smiles to veil his grief; nor knew,
How little they resemble those, that spring
From gentle impulses of hearts at ease.

For

For Jonadab, with penetrating eye,
Quickly difcern'd the grief, he ftrove to hide.
What caufe, faid he, can Amnon have to mourn?
A King's fon now,—a King in time may be.
Was it in probability, that I
Should be a King, the very contemplation
Would fhut my foul to forrow. Oh! the thought
Swells my imagination. Did but Amnon
Afpire as much to greatnefs, I could plot
Surprizing ftratagems. But he poor Prince
Has long imbib'd fuch clofe contracted notions,
As bar his path to honour. Like a maid
He talks of virtue, weeps at others woes,
Yet talks of greatnefs too; 'tis in the foul,
He fays, all greatnefs dwells; 'tis not the crown,
That makes his father great, but 'tis his virtues;
And thofe alone he wifhes to inherit,
Thereby to gain dominion o'er himfelf,
And reign unenvi'd; but perchance there now
Springs in his foul fome change of fentiment;
And he his principles, fo long retain'd,
Loth to renounce, may want a friend to prompt,
And urge him to the attainment of his will.
Then who fo fit for fuch a tafk as I?
I'm great in his efteem, have free accefs

To him at all times; but, if now I'm slack,
Perhaps I may be rivall'd in his favour
By some more forward to promote his wish.
I'll to him straight, in these cool ev'ning hours
Into his private garden he retires,
Sighs to the winds, and to the moon complains.
But I must him approach with seeming awe,
As fearful to disturb his solitude,
And with a gentle flow of soothing words
Insinuate myself into his soul,
Then guide him as I please.   The love-sick youth
Beneath the thickest solitary shade
Was wand'ring, lost in melancholy mood,
So deep in thought, he ne'er perceiv'd th' approach
Of Jonadab, till startled by his voice;
Then smil'd, as usual, as his friend drew near,
Who thus the Royal youth address'd—Oh! why
Dost thou, a King's son, pine in discontent?
Can there be ought, that's unattainable
To crown thy soul with peace?   Thy father's kind,
Too fond and too indulgent to refuse
A son's request, be what it will methinks.
But why from me conceal thy griefs? am I
A friend, unworthy of thy confidence?
Have I e'er been unfaithful to my trust?

Or

Or has some jealous whisperer impos'd
Upon my Royal friend's credulity,
To vilify his faithful Jonadab?
Half lost in thought, the Prince made no reply,
And Jonadab a while suspended stood;
But, recollecting, took his hand and said;
Why weeps my Prince? what sorrow wounds thy heart?
I love, says Amnon; and his hand withdrew
To wipe his tears, and turn'd from Jonadab:
Then seems returning, then he onward goes
In pensive sadness. Jonadab pursues,
Resolv'd to urge his full confession, lest
Some other should be made his confidant,
And he discarded, lose the Prince's favour.
Amnon return'd, as ready to confess
As he to hear, and thus his speech began.
O friend, I love—I love thee as my friend,
And such thou art, the sharer of my joys;
All my delights were doubled, shar'd with thee.
But now a strange dilemma has befall'n me;
I would not speak it to an ear but thine;
I love my sister Tamar; tell it not,
My reason almost fails to be my guide.
This passion, Oh! this wild rebellious passion,
If cherish'd, fast it grows as noisome weeds,

And,

And, if fupprefs'd, ftill ftrengthens in the ftalk.
So let it ftrengthen, till, too ftrong for me,
I fink beneath its weight. But Jonadab,
Ne'er let the fecret pafs thy lips, for I
So much refpect and honour her I love,
That for the richeft diadem on earth
I would not give her pain; her heart's fo prone
To pity, it would burft in grief for me,
Did fhe but know the half I feel for her.
Then Jonadab, with feeming kind affection,
And tears of fympathy reply'd; kind Prince,
Diftruft me not, thy confidence I claim;
Thou know'ft the feelings of my friendly heart
Admit no reft, if Amnon is unhappy;
Shall David's meaneft fubjects fmile fecure
Beneath his prudent equitable fway,
Their leaft complaints regarded? and his fon
Repine without redrefs? It muft not be.
Amnon reply'd, I cannot thee diftruft,
And if thou know'ft a way to eafe my heart,
Difcover it my friend, for I defpair.
Difpel thofe ufelefs tears, fays Jonadab:
Think not to drown it in thofe briny floods;
Love is a flame thofe waters cannot quench;
Nor is there any cure fhort of enjoyment.
Then

Then there's no hope for me, the Prince reply'd,
Till the kind earth receive me; for can I?
I cannot—Oh! I cannot injure her.
Droop not, my gentle friend, says Jonadab;
This tim'rous tenderness but ill becomes
A Royal Prince, the hope of Israel,
The son of David; think but who thou art,
The eldest son of Israel's mighty King;
Whose dreaded name thro' all the nations round
Strikes terror to his enemies, and fills
The grateful hearts of all his friends with joy;
Whose tongues with pleasure tell his mighty deeds,
And virgins celebrate his fame in songs;
While Amnon thus effeminately weeps,
Like some fair captive maid, snatch'd from the arms
Of her fond lover. O my Royal friend,
Better ten thousand injur'd virgins mourn,
Than David's son thus live inglorious.
There is a sort of viand she prepares,
Unparallel'd, of which none other knows
The just proportion of ingredients us'd.
A sickness feign'd might veil the deep design,
And put her in thy power; by this excuse
That thou canst take nought else; nor fear but she
Will keep the secret, to preserve her fame.

After

After a little paufe the youth reply'd,
It fhall be fo;—but yet I doubt—I fear—
If I—I'll think no more of confequences,
I am determin'd—yes, it fhall be fo.
To-morrow be it done, faid Jonadab.
Amnon reply'd—to-morrow is the day.
So parted they that night; and Jonadab,
In confcious pride of felf-fufficiency,
Thus to himfelf his Royal friend derides.
Poor thing, how eafily he's wrought upon?
In time the kingdom will be his, and I,
In fact, fhall reign, though he the title bears.
That time might be anticipated, but
Amnon wants courage for fo bold a ftroke.
He's unambitious, nor has refolution
To feize a tempting crown within his reach;
But fhould it gently fall upon his head,
Perhaps he'll wear it, if fome bolder hand
Don't fnatch it off. But this Amour may prove
A clew to guide to greater enterprizes.
When thefe precife ones once extend beyond
The bounds their narrow minds have circumfcrib'd,
From ftep to ftep infenfibly they go,
Till fo familiariz'd by cuftom, they
With calmnefs will tranfact the very things,
Which

Which but to mention, ere they launch'd so far,
They'd shudder at. But I must wait th' event.
So saying, he retir'd to take repose,
The common blessing graciously diffus'd
Through Nature, to refresh her wearied sons;
That with new strength and vigour they may hail
The rising day, rejoicing in the light.

CANTO II.

FROM Amnon's wasted cities, with the crown
Of Hanun, their proud contumacious King,
Whose insolence had caus'd his overthrow,
The conquering King of Israel return'd
In glorious triumph to Jerusalem;
There from exhausting toils of bloody war
In safety to repose his wearied soul,
And taste the sweets of calm domestic bliss.
But ere the tumults of triumphal joy
Subsided, and the sacred rites perform'd
Of general praises with the harp and song,
The King's long-wish'd tranquility's disturb'd
By the sad news, that Amnon, his dear son,
A captive now to dang'rous sickness lies,
While life and death dispute their doubtful right.
The pious King laid down his harp, the song
Unfinish'd, and with anxious haste repair'd
To Amnon, whose dissimulation pass'd
Quite unsuspected. How could he suspect
A fraud of such sort in a virtuous son?
Full oft a partial parent overlooks
An obvious fault, or by affection blind

Discerns it not; but here no cause appear'd
T' awake suspicion, for his languid eyes
And palid cheeks gave signals of disease.
While thus the son in feeble tone complain'd,
The tender father stooping low to hear,—
I'm very sick, and whatsoever food
My servants here prepare, gives me disgust.
My sister Tamar, with superior skill,
Prepares a cake delicious to my taste;
This I could eat methinks from her kind hand,
Was she permitted to attend me here.
The King with fond solicitude retir'd,
And speedily dispatch'd a messenger
To Tamar, saying, 'twas his royal will,
That she should go direct to Amnon's house,
And there administer, with friendly aid,
Whate'er his sickly appetite demands.
The hour had pass'd, at which the royal maid
Came from her closet, splendidly attir'd;
Her hair with precious sparkling gems beset,
Faint mimicks of her more illustrious eyes.
About her neck a shining golden chain,
And o'er her loosely thrown, in careless folds,
A various colour'd robe, which, as she mov'd,
Trail'd on the ground, or flutter'd in the wind.
                              Thus

Thus all the virgin daughters of the King
In splendid raiment shone; but none so bright
In beauty, as the daughter of Maacah.
Soon as the sun had drank the morning dew,
Into her garden walk'd the lovely fair;
Not like a proud imperious haughty Queen,
With tossing head and scornful eyes, that glar'd
Malignant, scattering discontent around,
And vain in fancied greatness. Greater she
In inoffensive modesty, and bright
In virtue, as the rays that gild the morn,
Warming the flow'rs to ripeness, and exhaling
Their various sweets to fill the garden air.
Pleas'd with the grateful smell, she skips about
From flow'r to flow'r, and cautiously selects
The sweetest in a wreath, to deck that breast,
Which never yet inflam'd by vicious thought,
Or by unreasonable rebukes depress'd,
Had felt a secret pang, or learn'd to sigh.
But oh! how happy for the mortal race,
That from their eyes the future is obscur'd;
Did we but know the secret ills that wait
In darkness to surprize us, what would be
Our life, but one sad scene of misery?
All present pleasures would be bitter made

By

By aggravating thoughts of ills to come:
But blind to future things the present bless.
When peace and plenty smile auspiciously,
The heart with sense of Providence impress'd
O'erflows with gratitude, and conscious joy.
Such joy now fill'd the royal fair one's breast,
Intent on the formation of her wreath;
When lo! her handmaid came to her in haste,
With tidings, that a message had arriv'd
Straight from the King, declaring his desire,
That she to Amnon's house immediately
Would go, and dress him cakes, for he is sick.
The King's command she instantly obey'd;
Down dropt the unfinish'd wreath; she skimm'd along
O'er the parterres, nor stay'd to find the path.
Her sweeping garments gently brush'd the flow'rs;
The ripest shedding, strew'd the way she went
With variegated fragments. So the breeze
Whisks o'er the forest, and some shatt'ring leaves
Fall gently rustling thro' the shrubs beneath.
Then, gath'ring up her robe, she onward sprang,
And sisterly affection urg'd her haste.
Amnon in highest expectation lyes
Counting the slow-pac'd moments as they pass'd;
Now thinks his scheme's discover'd—he's betray'd—

Or

Or some curs'd intervening accident
Delays, perhaps prevents her coming. Thus
Doubts, fears, and wild impatience in his breast
Tumultuously contended, till she came,
With all the feelings of a tender sister;
But not a thought of vile licentious love
Profan'd her breast; to see him thus she wept,
But turning, wip'd her tears, suppress'd her grief,
And with officious haste the cakes prepar'd.
Wisdom has pow'r, like the meridian sun,
To hide all other brightness in its glare;
But virgin modesty, with winning smiles,
Shines a perpetual morning. So she shone
Serenely mild, nor knew her pow'r to please.
But oh! the graceful dignity of virtue
Unthinking captivates the worthy soul,
The feebly good with emulation fires,
And strikes the very libertines with awe.
So Amnon, aw'd to see her lovely form,
Became irresolute; and recantation
Stagger'd his purpose.—First he paus'd; then thus
Expostulating with himself he lay;
Oh! how can I despoil this lovely maid,
This fairest of the fair? I cannot—no—
I'll let her go untouch'd. But then must I

Still

Still pine in languishment, as heretofore;
And Jonadab will at my weakness laugh.
At last some wine he snatch'd, and eager drank
To drown his scruples, and to fire his soul.
Such aid the most abandoned oft require,
When unsuspecting innocence at once.
Tempts and forbids, more pow'rfully forbids,
Than the persuasive eloquence of speech.
But the defence, which innocence can boast
With tears and mild intreaties, is but weak,
When love and wine unite their frantick pow'rs,
And leaving virtue fainting in the rear,
Rush on impetuous.—Hapless Tamar thus
To lawless outrage falls th' unwilling prey.

CANTO III.

Heav'n gave to man superior strength, that he
The weaker sex might succour and defend;
But he that dares pervert this giv'n blessing,
To ruin and destroy their innocence,
Shall feel pursuing vengeance, nor escape
Her rod uplifted, nor avert the stroke.
Conviction's sword shall pierce him, and remorse
With all the tortures of the mind assail,
Till he a victim falls to grim despair;
Except repentance timely to his aid
Come with her tears, to sooth, to mitigate;
While her attendant hope extends a ray,
To point where mercy spreads her healing wings.
Nor e'en with this is vengeance satisfied,
She'll still pursue with some external ills,
Exhausted health and spirits;—drooping—drear,
An outcast of society he roams,
Alike discarded by his friends and foes;
Perhaps assassination proves his end.

   The hapless Amnon from his couch arose,
Inflam'd with hatred more than once with love.
Frantick with keen remorse and conscious guilt,

He

He rav'd—he ſtamp'd—when to him Jonadab
Came to congratulate him; but the Prince
Shot from his eyes a keen malignant glance,
That ſpoke diſpleaſure, and with threat'ning hand
Upheld, thus in an angry tone began:
Hence from my ſight, thou baſeſt, worſt of fiends,
Nor ever dare approach my preſence more.
Struck with this ſtrange reception, Jonadab
Step'd back, and bowing with reſpectful awe,
Said,—O my Prince, why am I thus diſcarded?
I ſtill remain thy well affected friend,
Ready to——prompt me, (interrupts the Prince)
To do ſome greater crime than I have done.
Curſe on thy inſtigations; to my heart,
To my unexperienc'd heart thou drilld'ſt a way
T' infuſe licentiouſneſs; and thou a friend?
Ere thou preſum'ſt to take that ſacred name,
Abandon thy baſe principles, and learn
'Tis virtue only conſtitutes a friend.
He paus'd—th' aſtoniſh'd Jonadab approach'd
Nearer to Amnon; beg'd him to reſume
His wonted calmneſs, but to hear him ſpeak.
I'll hear no more of thee, reply'd the Prince;
I'm loſt, I'm irrecoverably loſt:
What were the pains I felt to thoſe I feel?

An hell within me burns, and deep remorſe,
That never dying worm, now gnaws my ſoul;
And thou, my inſtigator. Villain, flee,
Leſt this my crime I complicate with murder.
Then Jonadab withdrew chagrin'd, and full
Of ran'crous malice; mutt'ring as he went,
Shall murder crown thy crime young man—it ſhall;
But thou the murder'd,—not the murderer.
I'll hence to Abſalom, the brother kind
Of this fair injur'd maid; he doubtleſs will
Avenge her wrongs, and ſhew himſelf a brother.
He has a noble, calm, undaunted ſpirit;
Deliberately reſolute, and fit
For ſuch an enterprize; and Jonadab
Shall not be ſlack to aggravate the crime,
And urge him on, or aid him, if requir'd.
But I muſt veil my real ſentiments
With counterfeited ſorrow, and obſerve
Each ſecret movement of his varying ſoul,
And ſympathiſe with him. Young Abſalom
Returning from the fields, where he had been
To view his teeming flocks, jocund and gay,
In all the ſprightlineſs of youth and beauty,
Upon his ſlow-pac'd mule rode gently on
In careleſs attitude, and ſmil'd to ſee

All

All nature smile around; when Jonadab,
With solitary gait, approach'd, then turn'd
Aside, as if to shun the Royal youth;
Which Absalom perceiving, stopp'd his mule,
And leaning on his neck, with courteous air
Thus Jonadab in gentlest tone addrefs'd:
What mean those solemn looks, that down-cast eye?
Now peace and plenty bless our happy land:
Joy should methinks extend its cheering ray
To ev'ry individual; but thou
Look'st half dejected, wand'ring in the fields
At this late hour; the day is in decline;
The shepherds to their folds have led their flocks,
And to their peaceful homes are hast'ning. Come,
Return with me, my friend, nor farther go;
If ought distress thee, hide it not from me,
I have an heart to feel for the distress'd;
An hand too ever ready to revenge
The wrongs impos'd by violence and injustice
Smile and be happy, said the Royal youth;
And rising from his leaning posture, look'd
So gracefully endearing and so kind,
That Jonadab thus ventur'd to begin:—
'Tis not for me to smile, most noble Prince,
While inconsolable and unredress'd,

Diſhonour'd Tamar weeps in bitter woe,
Diſhonour'd, and by whom? ſays Abſalom,
Name but the villain, vengeance on his head
Shall inſtant fall; this hand ſhall ſtrike the blow.
Earth, canſt thou bear the wretch's feet to touch
Thy ſurface, and not groan? Whoe'er he be,
The miſcreant ſhall not ſee to-morrow' ſun.
Too haſty, Prince, ſays Jonadab; be calm;
Recall the fatal ſentence; tis too much
To raiſe thine hand againſt a brother's life,
Thine elder brother——Brother, ſaid the Prince,
And is it poſſible my brother thus
Sould be deprav'd? my brother Amnon too?
O virtue, where doſt thou reſide, if not
In Amnon? but if he's thus loſt to ſhame,
It cancels all the duty that I owe him;
Henceforth ſhall intercourſe between us ceaſe,
Till I have form'd a ſcheme to be reveng'd;
Amnon ſhall die, and die by Abſalom.
Go Jonadab, go home, and ſecret keep
This purpoſe of my ſoul;—I'll be thy friend,
Said Abſalom.—Then, onward as he paſs'd,
Thus Jonadab congratulates himſelf:

 Oh! happy I, no ſooner have I loſt
The favour of one Prince, but I have gain'd

Ano-

Another; Abſalom is more aſpiring;
Not cool and paſſive, like the ſilly Amnon,
But pants to rule; he has a kingly ſpirit.
Once in his garden, as I lay conceal'd,
I heard him in ſoliloquy, " Oh! to reign—
" To wield a ſceptre and eſtabliſh laws;
" Oh! did the people ſeek to me for judgment,
" And Princes wait for my deciſive voice,
" Ere they the cauſe determin'd; could I hear
" The loud applauding multitude exclaim,
" Long live King Abſalom."—He's fit to rule.
When Amnon is diſpatch'd, perhaps he may
Aſſume the kingdom—Be it ſo, and I
Will be his ready agent, if he pleaſe,
To aid his plots, or form them. Oh! how ſweet
The counſel that is fram'd to pleaſe our wills,
How readily adopted; how deſpis'd
That which is adverſe, be it e'er ſo good.
But dear, dear ſelf ſtands firſt in the account
Of friends, and that's the friend I'll ever ſerve:
Whether to Amnon or to Abſalom
I pay external homage. If to me
This Abſalom proves too imperious,
I'll aid the King, and keep myſelf ſecure.
Ay—that's the centre to which I muſt point

All schemes and plots; then smiling as he went,
With eager pace he hasten'd to his home.
    Grief and revenge now labour'd in the breast
Of Absalom; but artfully he hides
The struggling passions; a composure feign'd,
Sits on his countenance with placid ease;
And he in seeming gaiety rode home.
His servants there in readiness attend,
Each anxious to receive the first command;
Nor fear unjust reproofs, nor angry frowns,
Th' unwelcome greetings of imperious Lords.
Too oft do masters, void of judgment, check,
By froward peevishness and discontent,
The many little assiduities,
Which otherwise a servant's zeal would mark,
Nor make distinction between good and bad;
But Absalom, with nicest judgment, scans
Their merits and defects; he in reproof
Is slowly cautious, and exactly just;
No clam'rous oaths re-eccho thro' his hall,
Nor mutt'ring servants whisper imprecations;
Tho' affable and courteous, yet he ne'er
To low familiarity descends;
But with great dignity is nobly kind,
Reigns in their hearts, and by enliv'ning smiles
En-

Encourag'd, they spontaneously attend,
And love completes their servitude with joy.
So now, as always at their lord's approach,
A secret transport thrill'd thro' ev'ry heart.
The gate one open'd, one receiv'd the mule,
Whilst he dismounting with a sprightly bound,
Tripp'd lightly o'er the pavement; and those eyes
Which ever spread serenity around,
Sparkled with seeming pleasure till he came,
Ent'ring his mansion, to where Tamar sat
In the most striking attitude of woe;
Her head, bestrew'd with ashes and reclin'd,
One trembling hand supported; th' other hid
Among the fragments of her robe, which she
In the first agonies of her grief had torn.
He stopp'd, turn'd pale; then in his changing face
Resentment flush'd, and sorrow swell'd his heart,
Which lab'ring to suppress he trembling stood;
But like a torrent, which breaks down a bank
New rais'd to stop its course, so burst his grief
Thro' all his feign'd composure. In his arms
He clasp'd the grieving fair, and mutual tears
Proclaim'd the anguish of their burden'd hearts.
But tho' his sorrow thus had burst its bounds,
Revenge in ambush lurk'd, while thus the Prince

With

With foothing words his fifter thus addrefs'd,—
I know the fad occafion of thy woe;
But he's thy brother; filent bear thy wrongs,
Nor by immod'rate grief enhance the ill
Which cannot be redrefs'd. No blame is thine;
My fifter ftill in heart is undefil'd.
Tamar attempts reply; but from their fprings
In fwifter currents flow'd the briny pearls;
At length the pow'r of fpeech return'd, the fair
Heav'd a deep figh, and thus her moan began,—
O injury unparallel'd! O deed
More cruel than the murd'rers deadly blow!
He takes our life, 'twas lent but for a time;
Perhaps fome years—perhaps a day—an hour:
But he that robs a woman of her honour,
Robs her of more than life;—a brother too
Still aggravates the guilt.—O purity,
Thou firft of female charms, to thee we owe
Our dignity; which, if in meeknefs clad,
Gives us infuperable pow'r; but, if
Of this depriv'd, our moft prefumpt'ous claim
Is cool compaffion. O dejected ftate!
That humble homage we receive from men,
In fuch proportion as our virtue fails,
Diminifhes. Th' ineftimable gem,

More

More precious than fine gold or rubies,—far
Outvies the dazzling rays of beaut'ous forms,
Which like gay meteors but excite our gaze,
Then fade away. But this pre-eminence
No more I boast; now stamp'd with infamy,
That due respect, that def'rence ever paid
To my exalted state shall hence be chang'd
To scorn: tho' by the dignity of birth
Protected from low insult, can I 'scape
The meaning leer, the vain contemptuous smile,
Or the more humbling pity of the proud?
Such moving strains in Absalom call'd forth
All the fond raptures of fraternal love;
Who thus consol'd her grief,—thou ne'er shall be
Abandon'd to the scorn of taunting dames,
Who triumph in the downfal of the fair.
My home be ever thine; in me behold
Thy guardian, brother, friend, companion kind.
'T shall be my earliest and my latest care,
With chearful converse to enliv'n thy hours;
All thou canst wish, which I have pow'r to grant,
Expect from me. His sister gave her hand,
An earnest of conformity—he press'd
The giv'n pledge; her grateful heart reply'd,—
O brother, always kind, now doubly so,

         To

To ope thy friendly arms in this diſtreſs,
And take me to protection: I accept
Thy offer'd boon. Farewell, ye courtly ſcenes;
No more ſhall Tamar ſhine in your reſorts;
But here recluſe and tranquil ever 'bide;
Regaling in that never-cloying feaſt,
Th' internal calm of an untainted mind.
This none can raviſh from me; this is life.
That God which rais'd my father to the throne,
And ſtill protects him with his pow'rful arm,
Shall be my all in all. To him I'll pray
Inceſſant, and the great Jehovah's name
Shall fire my theme, and fill my heav'nly ſong.

CANTO IV.

Now solemn evening drew her silent veil
O'er smiling nature, and the pious King
In supplication spent the sacred hour
With special fervour, making intercession
To the great sole dispenser of all good
To bless his son, and soon restore his health.
He scarce had ended prayer, when tidings came
That Jonadab beg'd audience.—The King
Eager to learn, thus instantly reply'd,
Go send him hither; welcome to my soul
Is Jonadab, my Amnon's social friend;
He doubtless comes to bring me news of him.
He enters.—Thus the King,—O Jonadab,
How does thy friend, my son, my Amnon now?
Amnon is well, O King, says Jonadab.
Is well! return'd the astonish'd King, is well!
'Tis but few hours since I myself him saw,
And saw him sick,—and say'st thou now he's well;
Thou know'st it not, which much I wonder at,
Because I know he loves thee; go now to him,
Go act a friendly part, go comfort him,
I tell thee he is sick.—Says Jonadab,

        I can

I can inform thee of the whole device
Of his pretended sickness. Then the King,—
Say'st thou pretended sickness? If there is
Dissimulation in my son, declare it;
I'll hear thee;—but take heed thou slander not,
Nor censure him unjustly, on thy life.
Amnon has not been sick, says Jonadab;
'Twas but a feint to lure his sister there
To his embraces, and he has succeeded.
What do I hear? reply'd the King; my son
Defil'd my daughter! Rising as he spoke,
With indignation flashing from his eyes:
Forth from his house he rush'd with hasty steps
To Amnon, who was unprepar'd to see
This unexpected visitant: The youth
Already self-convicted, now abash'd,
Ne'er ventur'd once to raise his down-cast eyes,
But speechless and confounded stood to hear
His sharp rebuke; when thus the King began:—
O son, thou shameful troubler of my house;
What hast thou done? Where are thy princely virtues
Inculcated so long? Now blasted all.
My elder-born, my first, my greatest joy,
Thus to debase thyself, thou that should'st be
The first in virtue, as the first in birth.

How

How can a Prince, himself debas'd with crimes,
Aspire to judge and punish wicked men?
In which of all my sons can I confide,
Now Amnon fails, whom I have faultless deem'd?
Thou bitter herb,—thou blemish of my honour;
How can I brook this foul disgrace? Must I
For ever bear confusion in my face,
And blush for thee, thou worse than enemy?
Amnon, no longer able to support
Such just reproof, in silence turn'd away,
And bursting into tears withdrew.—The King
Return'd with anger burning in his breast,
Mingled with sorrow for his daughter's wrongs;
My daughter! Oh! my daughter! he exclaim'd,
I would avenge thy wrongs; but oh! if I
Avenge my daughter, I destroy my son.
Then, all a father's tenderness prevail'd,
He wept,—his wrath subsided and he paus'd,
His own past failings rising in his mind;
His guilty love for Bathsheba—he sigh'd
Her murder'd husband; shudd'ring at the thought,
He saw no way to sooth the present ills
But suff'ring and forbearance.—Then the King,
As if the stroke came from the hand of Heav'n,
Fell prostrate to the earth, submitting thus:

Right-

Righteous art thou, O Lord, and all thy judgments juſt.
Amnon mean while, with piercing grief oppreſs'd,
Doubled by th' ſore diſpleaſure of the King,
Sat down and wept, while tears ſupply'd their ſtreams.
Then riſing, walk'd about with reſtleſs ſteps,
And thus in bitter agonies complain'd:
What am I now, and where? Of late I pin'd
In hopeleſs love, yet then I had ſome ſtay,
An heart-felt innocence, that could ſupport
And cheer the drooping ſpirits. But alas!
Virtue has left me now, and I'm expos'd;
Expos'd to what? to what, alas! I know not;
'Tis Hell itſelf burſts in upon my ſoul,
And pours forth all its torments.—Terrors! Death!
O irrecoverable innocence!
Where art thou gone? for ever baniſh'd hence.
Ariſe ye thickeſt miſts, ye darkeſt clouds
O'er-caſt thoſe twinkling ſtars. O ſable night,
Wrap me in deepeſt ſhades, nor let a beam
Of penetrating light expoſe me more;
Darkneſs is fitted to the guilty mind
That ſhrinks and ſtarts at ev'ry glimmering ray.
But oh! it is not in the pow'r of darkneſs
To hide the hated ſelf from ſelf; within
A ſacred light perpetually ſhines,

Ex-

Expoſing ev'ry failure to the ſenſe,
That vainly ſtruggles to compoſe the mind,
And huſh her ſad inquietudes to peace.
But peace, the gueſt of innocence alone,
Takes an eternal leave when guilt intrudes,
And now has took eternal leave of me.
Ah! wretched me! Oh! curſe on vicious friends!
Had Jonadab advis'd me virtuouſly,
I'd ſtill been innocent, and Tamar pure;
My father ſtill had ſmil'd on me with joy,
Nor had I trembled at his chiding frowns;
Abſalom would have call'd me brother ſtill,
But now he'll own me not.—This flight is juſt,
And this the leaſt part of my puniſhment;
For inward guilt has yet ſeverer pangs.
So wander'd he, complaining half the night,
Then ſought for reſt in ſleep, but ſought in vain:
Terrific dreams invade his wiſh'd repoſe;
He ſleeps, ſtarts, wakes;-then ſleeps and ſtarts again;
And riſes ſoon, but not to meet the morn
With joy as heretofore; but to bewail
The loſs of that ſweet calm that ever dwells
Within the guiltleſs breaſt; and in the world
Dwells no one more entitled to the bliſs
That waits on virtue, than was Amnon once:

He therefore more severely feels the loss
For having tasted in its first degree
Its sov'reign blessedness.—Who'd then forsake
The peaceful path of virtue to pursue
Alluring vice through folly's labyrinth,
Grasping at shadows of felicity,
'Till overtaken by her evil train
Of shame, remorse, confusion, and despair?
Such evils now the hapless Amnon haunt,
While in th' avenging hand of Absalom
Death lurking lies.—Th' ambitious Prince, resolv'd
At once t' avenge his sister, and remove
An obstacle betwixt him and the crown,
With unremitting vigilance attends
The silent shades and unfrequented paths
Where Amnon used to walk, and meditate,
Hoping to meet defenceless and alone
The destin'd youth, and steal away his life.
But Amnon now as cautiously avoids
His dreaded presence; not with dread of death;
Such fear ne'er fill'd his unsuspicious breast;
But conscious guilt, that daunter of the soul,
That few can brave, deter'd the timid youth.
Two years within the breast of Absalom
Revenge in ambush lurk'd, while in his face

The

The mildeſt gentleneſs and ſweetneſs play'd:
Thus ſecret burns the ſubterraneous fire,
While on earth's teeming ſurface gaily ſmiles
The verdant herbage ſtrew'd with various flowers,
Till, burſting from beneath, the ſulph'rous fumes
O'erturn the mountains, and the crumbling mould
Buries the blooming beauties that it bore:
So he unable longer to contain
The hidden rancour burning in his breaſt
Determin'd by ſome bold and deſp'rate ſtroke
T' effect his purpoſe; and with Jonadab
Conſulted, who thus readily advis'd:—
Aſſume the friend,—entice him to thine houſe;
The cred'lous youth will ne'er ſuſpect a fraud.
Now is the time, now comes the yearly feaſt
When ſhepherds fleece their flocks: make him thy gueſt
With all thy brothers: when with mirth and wine
His heart's elate, how eaſy will it be
To give the final blow. With lowring brow
Revengeful Abſalom the raſh advice
Adopted, and a ſullen gloom o'ercaſt
His lively features.   Stern as that grim Lord
That through the foreſt takes his fearleſs way,
With high deportment Abſalom retir'd.

CANTO V.

Returning summer now came smiling on,
Exciting ev'ry peaceful breast to mirth;
But Amnon meets with tears the fatal season:
This sad remembrancer of his past crime
Awoke his grief, and from his couch he rose
Ere yet th' approaching day began to dawn,
While the full moon reign'd mistress of the night.
Sleep on, ye sons of innocence and ease,
(The restless Amnon with a sigh exclaim'd,
As from his window high he cast a look
Over the silent streets, for not a voice
Disturb'd the solemn hour) sleep on—sleep on:
So was I wont to sleep away the night,
Rise with the morn, and in the day rejoice:
But now in morn or night, or sleep or 'wake,
I feel no joy. Oh that I could forget
I once was happy! Oh that this one step,
One erring step, should kill my peace for ever.
O moon, I blush beneath thy silver beams;
I've oft beheld thee with exulting heart,
But now I shrink at ev'ry thing that's pure:
A modest virgin, innocent and fair,

Strikes

Strikes terror to my soul: to me she seems
Exalted high above my fallen state:
If such and one I venture to approach,
I instantly recoil, and justly pay
A secret adoration to the breast
Of innocence; for Oh! what parity
Can there subsist 'twixt innocence and guilt?
The world's reproaches and censorious sneers
Harrow the heart and aggravate the sense:
But yet that aggravation poiz'd against
The pangs of guilt, is of but little weight;
The world offended may again be won,
Or all its vain reproaches set at nought,
When the heart, firmly steel'd with innocence,
Shrinks not, but rises with true nobleness,
Superior to the grov'ling sons of vice
And smiles at pow'rless envy.—But alas!
To me returns, whether of day or night,
Aid sharp reflection and new point its spears.
Now waking birds in chearful concert join;
Their ev'ry note proclaims them innocent.
The sun arises and the world awakes;
The Prince retires with melancholy steps
Into his garden, where recluse and still
Beneath the arching boughs of shady trees,

With head declin'd and arms lock'd round his breast.
He sigh'd the heavy slow-pac'd hours away;
'Till interrupted by a messenger,
Who, with due deference approaching near,
Thus spake: O Prince, I come from Absalom,
His sheep he sheers to-morrow, and intreats
Thee, with thy Royal brothers, to partake
The feast, and spend with him the day in mirth.
Surprize and pleasure rush'd into his heart
At such an unexpected invitation,
Which he accepted nor did hesitate
One moment to resolve; for Amnon still
Was unspicious as an infant child,
That fearless trusts itself to ev'ry arm
That open's to receive it. With quick step
He paces to and fro; his bosom glows,
And thus anticipates th' expected bliss.
O joyful day when I again shall meet
My dear offended brother, whom so long
I've cautiously avoided; his good will
Greatly exceeds my most advent'rous hope:
Forgetful of my faults, he kindly now
Invites me to his house, without reproach
Or intimation of my late misdeeds.
Yes, my good brother, I will be thy guest—

My

My grateful Heart o'erflows; I now could fall
Down at thy feet, and from thy hand receive
The death I do deserve.   Thus Amnon still,
In humble strain and true repentant heart,
Pour'd forth his soul in such soliloquies
All day and night, till in the morning fair,
The foremost of the princely cavalcade,
He gladly hastened to the fatal feast.
Now Absalom with secret pleasure sees
The long wish'd day arrive, and in the morn
Assiduously in comely dress array'd
His lovely person, lovely in extreme:
Not in all Israel's num'rous tribes was found
His peer in beauty; for from head to foot
No blemish, no deformity, was seen;
But well proportion'd limbs, and features fair,
With ev'ry natural, ev'ry borrow'd grace
That gives to beauty power.   The conscious Prince
Omitted no external ornament
That might, if possible, such gifts improve:
But looking at his spotless hands, he said,—
Must these be dy'd in blood? a brother's blood?
No, I have servants, they shall give the blow.
Then to and fro he through his chamber stalk'd,

Revolving in his mind the confequence
Of op'ning his defign. He paus'd, he thought
His fervants might refufe—or worfe, betray.
At length he fays,—I'm wrong to cenfure them;
Great proofs I've had of their fidelity;
I'll truft them now. Then call'd he thofe he lov'd;
They came. He fays, You have done all things well
According to my order for this feaft,
But on your cares I can fo well depend,
That whatfoever is given to your charge
I think no more of, for I've always found
You true and faithful; therefore I make choice
Of you for my accomplices this day:
'Tis not intended for a day of mirth,
As it appears, and muft as yet appear
Till I've fulfill'd the purpofe of my foul.
Our guefts muft fumptuoufly be entertain'd:
But when they have partook the rich repaft,
And wine exhilerates and mirth prevails,
Be you prepar'd, and when I give the word,
Pierce Amnon to the heart, for he muft die.
His fervants tremble at the dire command.
Why tremble ye? faid Abfalom, fear not,
'Tis I command you—all the deed is mine;

Ye

Ye are but inftruments within my grafp,
And of his blood are fpotlefs: if there's guilt
In taking vengeance for the attrocious crime,
Let all that guilt be mine: fince juftice fleeps
In his fond father's hand, 'tis right that I
Affume the pow'r, and on his impious head
Hurl vengeance. But obferve, it next behoves
Us to evade the ftorm that will enfue:
In Gefhur we fhall find a fafe retreat:
My fleeteft horfes for the flight prepare:
Soon as the wound is given we'll mount and flee;
Swift as the fweeping winds we'll o'er the hills,
And leave the King to bury him, and mourn.
His fervants, more by love than duty bound,
All bow'd obedient to his fov'reign will.
Now came the Royal guefts, and Amnon firft
Difmounting from his mule, with confcious blufh
And fault'ring voice thus ventur'd to addrefs
Th' offended brother:—O my Abfalom,
Forgive, he faid—and interrupting tears
Pleading more pow'rfully than eloquence,
Stagger'd the purpofe of Maacah's fon,
And in his feeling foul a conflict rais'd
Betwixt his brother's life and fifter's fame:

He

He silent paus'd; but in his breast revenge
Was too deep rooted by a too year's growth
For one soft moment to eradicate:
He therefore wip'd away a piteous tear,
And made to Amnon this compos'd reply:
I did not send for thee to weep and mourn:
To-day I have a feast; this prosp'rous year
Increasing flocks increase the shepherds joy:
Rojoice with me, my brother and be glad.
Then did he warmly press his hand, and point
The chiefest place. The Prince shed tears of joy,
Then sat him down, forgot his grief and smil'd.
Wine in profusion sparkled in the bowls,
Inspiring social mirth; they freely quaff'd;
But Absalom th' emolient draught evades,
Lest it relax his stern determination;
But quick replenishes the sinking bowls,
Pressing on all the intoxicating cup,
'Till mirth predominates, and ev'ry heart
Expands with social freedom; Absalom
Then gives the fatal word; his servants plunge
The destin'd dart, and from the Prince's side
Gush'd forth life's reeking stream—he fell—uprose
In consternation those whom vengeance spar'd,

         Each

Each trembling for his life; confus'd they fled:
Mingling with gore, the wine in currents flow'd;
While, rolling in the flood, the murder'd Prince
Alone, in all the agonies of woe,
Groan'd out his ſoul, and clos'd his eyes in death.

F I N I S.

APPENDIX.

CONTAINING

PASTORALS, &c.

A POEM,

On the Suppofition of an Advertifement appearing in a Morning Paper, of the Publication of a VOLUME *of* POEMS, *by a* SERVANT MAID.

THE tea-kettle bubbled, the tea things were fet,
The candles were lighted, the ladies were met;
The how d'ye's were over, and entering buftle,
The company feated, and filks ceas'd to ruftle:
The great Mrs. Confequence open'd her fan;
And thus the difcourfe in an inftant began:
(All affected referve, and formality fcorning,)
I fuppofe you all faw in the paper this morning,
A Volume of Poems advertis'd—'tis faid
They're produc'd by the pen of a poor Servant Maid.
A fervant write verfes! fay's Madam Du Bloom;
Pray what is the fubject?—a Mop, or a Broom?
He, he, he,–fay's Mifs Flounce; I fuppofe we fhall fee
An Ode on a Difhclout—what elfe can it be?

> Says

Says Miſs Coquettilla, why ladies ſo tart?
Perhaps Tom the Footman has fired her heart;
And ſhe'll tell us how charming he looks in new clothes,
And how nimble his hand moves in bruſhing the ſhoes;
Or how the laſt time that he went to May-Fair,
He bought her ſome ſweethearts of ginger-bread ware.
For my part I think, ſays old lady Marr-joy,
A ſervant might find herſelf other employ:
Was ſhe mine I'd employ her as long as 'twas light,
And ſend her to bed without candle at night.
Why ſo? ſays Miſs Rhymer, diſpleas'd I proteſt
'Tis pity a genius ſhould be ſo depreſt!
What ideas can ſuch low-bred creatures conceive,
Says Mrs. Noworthy, and laught in her ſleeve.
Says old Miſs Prudella, if ſervants can tell
How to write to their mothers, to ſay they are well,
And read of a Sunday the Duty of Man;
Which is more I believe than one half of them can;
I think 'tis much *properer* they ſhould reſt there,
Than be reaching at things ſo much out of their ſphere.
Says old Mrs. Candour, I've now got a maid
That's

That's the plague of my life—a young goſſipping
    jade;
There's no end of the people that after her come,
And whenever I'm out, ſhe is never at home;
I'd rather ten times ſhe would ſit down and write,
Than goſſip all over the town ev'ry night.
Some whimſical trollop moſt like, ſays Miſs Prim,
Has been ſcribbling of nonſenſe, juſt out of a whim,
And conſcious it neither is witty or pretty,
Conceals her true name, and aſcribes it to Betty.
I once had a ſervant myſelf, ſays Miſs Pines,
That wrote on a Wedding, ſome very good lines:
Says Mrs. Domeſtic, and when they were done,
I can't ſee for my part, what uſe they were *on;*
Had ſhe wrote a receipt, to've inſtructed you how
To warm a cold breaſt of veal, like a ragou,
Or to make cowſlip wine, that would paſs for
    Champaign;
It might have been uſeful, again and again.
On the ſofa was old lady Pedigree plac'd,
She own'd that for poetry ſhe had no taſte,
That the ſtudy of heraldry was more in faſhion,
And boaſted ſhe knew all the creſts in the nation.
Says Mrs. Routella,—Tom, take out the urn,
And ſtir up the fire, you ſee it don't burn.

The tea things remov'd, and the tea-table gone,
The card-tables brought, and the cards laid thereon,
The ladies ambitious for each others crown,
Like courtiers contending for honours sat down.

A POEM,

On the Suppoſition of the Book having been publiſhed and read.

THE dinner was over, the table-cloth gone,
The bottles of wine and the glaſſes brought on,
The gentlemen fill'd up the ſparkling glaſſes,
To drink to their king, to their country and laſſes:
The ladies a glaſs or two only requir'd,
To th' drawing-room then in due order retir'd;
The gentlemen likewiſe that choſe to drink tea;
And, after diſcuſſing the news of the day,
What wife was ſuſpected, what daughter elop'd,
What thief was detected, that 'twas to be hop'd,
The raſcals would all be convicted, and rop'd;
What chambermaid kiſs'd when her lady was out;
Who won, and who loſt, the laſt night at the rout;

What

What lord gone to France, and what tradesman
    unpaid,
And who and who danc'd at the last masquerade;
What banker stopt payment with evil intention,
And twenty more things much too tedious to
    mention.
Miss Rhymer says, Mrs. Routella, ma'am, pray
Have you seen the new book (that we talk'd of
    that day,
At your house you remember) of Poems, 'twas said
Produc'd by the pen of a poor Servant Maid?
The company silent, the answer expected;
Says Mrs. Routella, when she'd recollected;
Why, ma'am, I have bought it for Charlotte; the
    child
Is so fond of a book, I'm afraid it is spoil'd:
I thought to have read it myself, but forgat it;
In short, I have never had time to look at it.
Perhaps I may look it o'er some other day;
Is there any thing in it worth reading, I pray?
For your nice attention, there's nothing can 'scape.
She answer'd,—There's one piece, whose subject's
    a Rape.
A Rape! interrupted the Captain Bonair,
A delicate theme for a female I swear;

Then fmerk'd at the ladies, they fimper'd all round,
Touch'd their lips with their fans,—Mrs. Con-
    fequence frown'd.
The fimper fubfided, for fhe with her nods,
Awes thefe lower affemblies, as Jove awes the gods.
She fmil'd on Mifs Rhymer, and bad her proceed—
Says fhe, there are various fubjects indeed:
With fome little pleafure I read all the reft,
But the Murder of Amnon's the longeft and beft.
Of Amnon, of Amnon, Mifs Rhymer, who's he?
His name, fays Mifs Gaiety's quite new to me:—
'Tis a Scripture tale, ma'am,—he's the fon of
    King David,
Says a Reverend old Rector: quoth madam, I
    have it;
A Scripture tale?—ay—I remember it—true;
Pray is it i'th' old Teftament or the new?
If I thought I could readily find it, I'd borrow
My houfe-keeper's Bible, and read it to-morrow.
'Tis in Samuel, ma'am, fays the Rector:—Mifs
    Gaiety
Bow'd, and the Reverend blufh'd for the laity.
You've read it, I find, fays Mifs Harriot Anderfon;
Pray, fir, is it any thing like Sir Charles Grandifon?
How you talk, fays Mifs Belle, how fhould fuch a
    girl write   A novel,

A novel, or any thing elfe that's polite?
You'll know better in time, Mifs:—She was but
    fifteen:
Her mamma was confus'd—with a little chagrin,
Says,—Where's your attention, child? did not
    you hear
Mifs Rhymer fay, that it was poems, my dear?
Says Sir Timothy Turtle, my daughters ne'er look
In any thing elfe but a cookery book:
The propereft ftudy for women defign'd;
Says Mrs. Domeftic, I'm quite of your mind.
Your haricoes, ma'am, are the beft I e'er eat,
Says the Knight, may I venture to beg a receipt.
'Tis much at your fervice, fays madam, and bow'd,
Then flutter'd her fan, of the compliment proud.
Says Lady Jane Rational, the bill of fare
Is th' utmoft extent of my cookery care:
Moft fervants can cook for the palate I find,
But very few of them can cook for the mind.
Who, fays Lady Pedigree, can this girl be;
Perhaps fhe's defcended of fome family:—
Of family, doubtlefs, fays Captain Bonair,
She's defcended from Adam, I'd venture to fwear.
Her Ladyfhip drew herfelf up in her chair,
And twitching her fan-fticks, affected a fneer.

                               I know

I know something of her, says Mrs. Devoir,
She liv'd with my friend, Jacky Faddle, Esq.
'Tis sometime ago though; her mistress said then,
The girl was excessively fond of a pen;
I saw her, but never convers'd with her—*though*
One can't make acquaintance with servants, you
   know.
'Tis pity the girl was not bred in high life,
Says Mr. Fribbello:—yes,—then, says his wife,
She doubtless might have wrote something worth
   notice:
'Tis pity, says one,—says another, and so 'tis.
O law! says young Seagram, I've seen the book, now
I remember, there's something about a mad cow.
A mad cow!—ha, ha, ha, ha, return'd half the room;
What can y' expect better, says Madam Du Bloom?
They look at each other,—a general pause—
And Miss Coquettella adjusted her gauze.
The Rector reclin'd himself back in his chair,
And open'd his snuff-box with indolent air;
This book, says he, (snift, snift) has in the beginning,
(The ladies give audience to hear his opinion)
Some pieces, I think, that are pretty correct;
A stile elevated you cannot expect:
To some of her equals they may be a treasure,
         And

And country laffes may read 'em with pleafure.
That Amnon, you can't call it poetry neither,
There's no flights of fancy, or imagery either;
You may ftile it profaic, blank-verfe at the beft;
Some pointed reflections, indeed, are expreft;
The narrative lines are exceedingly poor:
Her Jonadab is a ——— the drawing-room door
Was open'd, the gentlemen came from below,
And gave the difcourfe a definitive blow.

WIT AND BEAUTY,

A PASTORAL.

CELIA.

Our shepherds are gone o'er the hill,
   To sport on the neighbouring plain;
Let's sit by this murmuring rill,
   And sing till they come back again.

SYLVIA.

We'll sing of our favourite swains,
   By whom our fond hearts are possest;
And Daphne shall judge of the strains,
   Which sings of her shepherd the best.

DAPHNE.

Come sing then, and Daphne will hear,
   Nor linger the time to prolong;
And this wreath of roses I wear,
   Shall crown the fair victor in song.

CELIA.

My Thirsis is airy and gay,
   His pride is in pleasing the fair;
He sings and drives sorrow away,
   His humour will banish all care.

SYLVIA.

To Daphnis the pride of my lay,
  The merits of beauty belong;
His smiles will chase sorrow away,
  As well as your shepherd's fine song.

CELIA.

When piping my Thirsis is seen,
  The virgins assemble around;
And all the blithe swains of the green,
  Approve, while they envy the sound.

SYLVIA.

When Daphnis approaches the plains,
  The virgins all blush with surprise;
With negligence treating their swains,
  And fix on my Daphnis their eyes.

CELIA.

If e'er I am pensive and sad,
  Or sigh to the evening gale;
I'm cheer'd by the voice of my lad,
  Who tells me a humorous tale.

SYLVIA.

When I am perplexed with fears,
  And nothing can give me delight;
As soon as my Daphnis appears,
  I languish away at the sight.

Daphne.

Now cease to contend, my dear lasses,
   My wreath I'll acknowledge your due;
Nor yet can I tell which surpasses,
   Your merits you equally shew.

'Twas Strephon that gave me the treasure,
   Which now I to you shall impart;
(That name! O, I speak it with pleasure!
   It ever enraptures my heart.)

Nor Sylvia, nor Celia, shall have it,
   I'll justly divide it in two;
Believe me, my Strephon, that gave it,
   Is beautiful, witty, and—true.

ABSENCE AND DEATH.

A PASTORAL.

WHEN ev'ry eye that knew no cause to weep,
And peaceful minds were hush'd in pleasing sleep,
Two virgin nymphs, whom Love had left forlorn,
Ne'er clos'd their weeping eyes, from eve to morn:
For Strephon's absence, Daphne's tears were shed,
And Hebe mourn'd her faithful Collin dead;
Their sorrows were not to each other known,
Alike they mourn'd, and silent was their moan;
Awhile they wept, 'till one the silence broke;
Thus Hebe answer'd, and thus Daphne spoke.

DAPHNE.

Say, gentle maid, whence spring thy anxious fears?
What inward sorrows prompt thy gushing tears?
Thy case thou safely may'st to me impart,
True to my trust, and faithful from the heart;
My grief, I will suspend awhile to hear
Thy tale, and shed a sympathetic tear,

HEBE.

And will not Daphne then her grief impart?
To tell the sorrow, is to ease the heart.

Say

Say first, why heaves thy breast that lab'ring sigh,
And Hebe will alternately reply;
The plaintive sounds shall die along the vales,
And neighb'ring hills resound the moving tales.

DAPHNE.

A shepherd's absence I am doom'd to mourn,
While rigid fate forbids him to return;
Perhaps, like me, he mourns his forc'd delay,
Perhaps some fairer maid may tempt his stay;
Awhile, with flattering gales of hope I steer,
Then, dash'd and shipwreck'd on the rock of fear.

HEBE.

Young Collin did my yielding heart subdue,
A forester he was, and he was true;
He vow'd his heart from me should never rove;
I heard with joy, and gave him love for love;
But my dear swain, my Collin's dead, and I
Now live, but only to despair, and die.

DAPHNE.

My shepherd is the choicest of the swains,
That climb the hills, or traverse o'er the plains;
His radiant eyes beam forth a milder ray,
Than the fair star, that leads the dawning day;
Nor are the flocks, that graze the plains, so fair
As the dear swain that makes those flocks his care.

HEBE.

HEBE.

My forester was comely to behold,
His looks were pleasing as the tale he told;
The frock he wore, was of a fresher green
Than the gay forests, where he oft was seen;
And stately he, among his fellow swains,
As the tall fir, that o'er the forest reigns.

DAPHNE.

How swift the seasons fly throughout the year,
How oft the spring returns without my dear;
Yet should some blisful hour, some distant spring,
My long-mourn'd Strephon to his Daphne bring;
One happy hour with him, wou'd far o'er-pay
All I have suffer'd by his long delay.

HEBE.

No gloomy phantom has my joys o'er-cast,
My hopes are wither'd by a deadly blast;
See the surrounding woods, how ev'ry tree
Has dropp'd its leaves, and seems to mourn with me;
Though spring will quickly re-adorn the grove,
Yet I can never hope to see my love.

A PASTORAL.

YOUNG Damon gay, a faithful-hearted swain,
Long sought fair Daphne's love, but sought in vain;
He often told her how sincere he lov'd,
As oft the nymph his ardent flame reprov'd;
While yet his passion labour'd in his mind,
He walk'd abroad his straying steeds to find;
Just then fair Laura went across the green,
Long time this nymph fair Daphne's friend had been;
The swain to meet her stept across the way;
She stopt to hear what Damon had to say.

DAMON.

Say, friendly maid, why wand'ring here alone?
Where is thy friend, the lovely Daphne gone?
Ah! has some rival led her to the grove?
And may I never hope for Daphne's love?

LAURA.

A shepherd's fav'rite dog long lost has been,
Fair Daphne found him wand'ring on the green;
Much does the shepherd-swain his loss deplore,
The nymph is gone the wand'rer to restore.

DAMON.

DAMON.

Ah, wretched Damon! doom'd to love in vain,
She loves the dog, she loves the shepherd-swain;
Oh Daphne! I'll to death thy loss deplore,
These lips shall ne'er salute a virgin more.

LAURA.

Despair not, Damon, of fair Daphne's love,
Thy vows repeated, may her pity move;
See, up yon hill ascends the maiden gay,
Thou may'st o'ertake her, Damon, haste away.

She said, and Damon turn'd his eyes around,
And saw the maid ascend the rising ground;
Swift are the feet of messengers, that bring
Glad news of conquests to their sov'reign King;
But up the steep more swiftly Damon came,
Love, urg'd by fear, has swifter wings than fame.
The lovely Daphne smil'd to see him run,
And thus the swain in humble suit begun:

DAMON.

Why Daphne here, from ev'ry friend apart?
What on this hill can charm thy virgin heart?
If down the other side thou would'st descend,
My lovely maid, permit me to attend.

DAPHNE.

DAPHNE.

Now spring with verdure ev'ry field adorns,
And birds are singing on the bloomy thorns,
Can such things fail to charm? but Damon say,
How did you know that I was come this way?

DAMON.

I walk'd abroad, my straying steeds to see;
But my fond heart was still pursuing thee;
They were my small, but thou my greater care,
O happy chance, that led me to my fair.

DAPHNE.

A shepherd's dog has long been gone astray,
I found him on the green the other day;
This fav'rite dog, the swain does much lament,
I'll lead him home, and give the swain content.

DAMON.

Why in such haste! the sun, my fair one, see,
Is yet as high as yonder lofty tree;
Those verdant meadows, where fresh daisies grow,
Invite our steps, my Daphne, shall we go?

The maid consented, making no reply;
What maid could such a small request deny?
A chrystal stream, in gentle murmurs glides
Along the valley, and the meads divides;

Along

Along the banks the verdant alders grow,
Their branches bending to the stream below;
The tender leaves that hung on ev'ry spray,
And hawthorn blossoms shew'd the month was May;
Flow'rs, of various hue, bedeck'd the shade,
And there young Damon led the tender maid:
Her slender waist no gaudy ribband bound,
But Damon's arm did form a circle round;
Soft were the whisp'rings of the western gale,
But with more softness Damon told his tale;
The pleasing tale the maid in silence heard,
But in her heart the gentle swain preferr'd;
Thus o'er one meadow they were quickly gone,
Yet still by pleasant meadows tempted on,
How soon the lovers moments pass away,
How soon, how soon, approach'd the close of day,
The sun departed, and the plains grew damp,
And rising Cynthia trimm'd her silver lamp;
No more the birds to charm the year aspir'd,
And wand'ring lovers from the plain retir'd;
The swain ne'er thought to go, his steeds to find,
The nymph forgot to leave her dog behind.

LOVE AND FRIENDSHIP.

A PASTORAL.

TWO nymphs to whom the pow'rs of verse belong,
Alike ambitious to excel in song,
With equal sweetness sang alternate strains,
And courteous echo told the list'ning plains;
That of her lover sung, this of her friend;
Ye rural nymphs and village swains attend.

CELIA.

O Love, soft sov'reign, ruler of the heart!
Deep are thy wounds, and pleasing is the smart;
When Strephon smiles the wint'ry fields look gay,
Cold hearts are warm'd, and hard ones melt away.

SYLVIA.

Through ev'ry scene of temp'ral bliss is there
A greater blessing than a friend sincere?
'Tis Corydon that bears that tender name,
And Sylvia's breast returns the gen'rous flame.

CELIA.

When happy I survey my Strephon's charms,
His beauty holds me faster than his arms,

My

My heart is in a flood of pleasures tofs'd,
I faint, I die, and am in raptures loft.

SYLVIA.

And what are all thefe tumults of the heart,
But certain omens of a future fmart?
In friendfhip we more folid comforts find,
It cheers the heart, nor leaves a fting behind.

CELIA.

Surely no lark in fpring was e'er fo glad
To fee the morn, as I to fee my lad;
At his approach all anxious griefs remove,
And ev'ry other joy gives place to love.

SYLVIA.

O happy I! with fuch a friend to live!
Our joys united double pleafure give;
Our inmoft thoughts with freedom we unfold,
And grief's no longer grief, when once 'tis told.

CELIA.

All that is lovely in my fwain I find,
But am to all his imperfections blind;
What have I faid? I furely do him wrong,
No imperfections can to him belong.

F 2 SYLVIA.

SYLVIA.

The faithful friend sees with impartial eyes,
Nor scorns reproof, but speaks without disguise;
Blind to all faults, the eager lover sues,
Friends see aright, and ev'ry fault excuse.

Then Daphne from beneath a hawthorn sprung,
Where she attentive sat to hear the song;
Her breast was conscious of the tender glow,
That faithful friends, in mutual friendship know;
Her tender heart, by love's impulses mov'd,
With ardour beat to sing the swain she lov'd;
With emulation fir'd, the conscious maid
Thus to the fair contending virgins said.

DAPHNE.

Blest Celia, happy in a lover dear;
Blest Sylvia, happy in a friend sincere;
But surely I am doubly blest to find,
At once a friend sincere, and lover kind;
My Thirsis is my friend, my friend I say
And who in love can bear a greater sway
Strephon must his superior power own,
Nor is he less sincere than Corydon.

A PASTORAL.

YOUNG Corydon, a blithesome swain,
   As ever tended sheep,
Upon the verdant banks of LEAM,
   Was wont his flock to keep.

One ev'ning when the rising Moon
   Was peeping in the flood,
And ev'ry bird that sings by day,
   Sat silent in the wood.

With dog and staff he took his way,
   And whistled as he went;
To gather up his straying ewes,
   Was all the shepherd meant.

And while he sought the meadows round,
   Where they were wont to stray,
A maid more lovely than his ewes,
   Came tripping o'er the way.

The sheep no longer fill'd his thoughts,
   The nymph was all his care;
And thus the gentle shepherd-swain,
   Address'd the tender fair.

CORYDON.

Why comes my nymph so late abroad,
   To wander in the vale;
To hear the murmuring of the flood,
   And see the moon shine pale?
Or is it an appointed hour
   To meet some happy swain?
For maids are seldom seen alone
   So late upon the plain.

PASTORA.

I've been a visit to a friend,
   That lives by yonder grove,
Where shepherds tell their tender tales,
   And list'ning virgins rove:
I with my friend conversing stood,
   Abstracted from all care,
The sun went down, and night drew on
   Before I was aware.

CORYDON.

The swains were surely all unkind,
   That such a maid as you
Should e'er be seen to walk alone,
   And in the ev'ning too:

Now

Now Corydon moſt gladly will
   Attend you if he may;
You ſee the moon is haſting on,
   Then why ſhould we delay?

He ſaid, and took her by the hand;
   O happy ſhepherd he!
Paſtora too was pleas'd as well
   As ſhepherdeſs could be.

The ſwain no longer ſought around,
   His ſtraying ewes to find:
O happy nymphs that live in plains,
   Where ſhepherds are ſo kind.

A PASTORAL.

As Thirsis and Daphne, upon the new hay
   Were seated, surveying the plain;
No guilt in their bosoms their joys to allay,
   Or give them a moment of pain.

Not Venus, but Virtue had made them her care,
   She taught them her innocent skill;
The swain knew no art, but to pleasure the fair
   That Nature had form'd to his will.

Inspired by love, on his pipe he did play;
   O Virtue! how happy the swain!
While sweet Robin-red-breast that perch'd on the
      spray,
   And Daphne was pleas'd with the strain.

How pleasing the prospect, how cooling the breeze;
   The sun shone delightfully 'round;
And apples half ripe, grew so thick on the trees,
   The boughs almost bent to the ground.

Thus happily seated, by sympathy bound,
   How pleasing the mutual chain;
When either is absent, the prospects around
   Display all their beauties in vain.   They

They sat till the mist that arose from the brook,
  Inform'd them the ev'ning was nigh;
The swain shook his head with a languishing look,
  And 'rose from his seat with a sigh.

His flute he disjointed, and silent a while
  He gaz'd on his maid with delight;
Then gave her his hand, she arose with a smile,
  He kiss'd her, and bid her good night.

OBSERVATION.

LET the vain avaricious with oaths safely bind,
  Lest either forgetfully rove;
The band of affection secureth the mind,
  When the wishes are centered in love.
If virtue alone is the guide of the will,
  Distrust has no right to be there;
The swain has no reason to doubt of his skill,
  And the fair one has nothing to fear.

A PASTORAL DIALOGUE.

DAMON.

O Theron, say what means that down-cast eye,
What new found grief has taught thy breast to sigh?
Has some intruding swain thy purpose crost?
Or has some favourite ewe her lambkin lost?
Assume thy wonted cheerfulness dear lad,
Or tell thy Damon why thou look'st so sad.

THERON.

Fresh as the spring, and fair as op'ning day,
My Jessy smil'd, and stole my heart away;
But when of love I did to her complain,
She scarcely smil'd, nor answer'd me again:
None e'er could think, but those that feel the smart,
So fair a form could hide so hard a heart.

DAMON.

Ah, silly swain! and was thy beauty made,
For the cool frowns of one false nymph to fade?
O Theron, Theron, scorn the power of love,
Forbid the tender impulses to move:
See how that bee forsakes the blooming may,
And leaves it for the next that comes this way.

THERON.

THERON.

Must I, like fickle Jessy, learn to slight?
Yes,—what my Damon says is always right.
See'st thou that nymph, beneath the shady tree?
She looks this way; I wish she look'd at me:
If e'er thy Theron should his heart transfer
From his lost Jessy, it must go to her.

DAMON.

O say no more—no more of her, my friend;
For she is mine—my Doris!—O suspend—
Suspend thy choice, my swain, till thou hast seen
The village maids assemble on the green;
And if you would your fickle heart transfer,
Then take your choice of all the rest but her.

THERON.

Why are you angry now, my friend, my swain!
Your own advice I'll give you back again:
O Damon, Damon, scorn the power of love;
Forego your nymph, your simile to prove:
Forsake her, as the bee forsakes the may,
And I will be the next that comes this way.

THIRSIS

THIRSIS AND DAPHNE.

A POEM.

My muse of Thirsis sings, and of the shade,
Where he, poor shepherd, with his Daphne stray'd:
On Dunsmore waste, there stands a shady grove,
The sweet recess of solitude and love;
Hazles on this, on that side elms are seen,
To shade the verdant path that leads between.
A rose, less lovely than young Thirsis gay,
Adorns the sprig that bends across the way;
The way that does with various flow'rs abound,
The gentle shepherd cast his eyes around ;
He sought a flower with Daphne to compare,
And thought the drooping lily seem'd less fair:
A flame as pure as that fair sacred light,
That shines between the hazle boughs at night,
Inspires the am'rous Thirsis' tender breast,
Which, by that light, has often been confess'd:
Soft was his speech, and languishing his eye,
When he approach'd his Daphne with a sigh;
No dark deceit did to his heart belong,
And flatt'ry was as foreign to his tongue;

       " I love,

" I love, says he, (and took her by the hand)
" And my poor wounded heart's at your command;
" For you I'm doom'd in love's fierce flames to burn;
" Be kind, my dear, and love me in return."
Thus said the swain, and paus'd a little while;
The fair one's answer was a silent smile:
To see her smile, he smil'd amidst his pain,
And thus pursu'd his gentle suit again.
" How long must I be toss'd 'twixt hope and fear,
" And tell my pain to your regardless ear?
" No more in silence hear me thus complain,
" Nor force those flatt'ring smiles, to hide disdain;
" But say you love, and end my anxious care,
" Or frown, and let me die in sad despair."

To hear him thus his ardent flame express,
Poor swain! she pity'd him; what could she less?
Her love, perhaps, at length may be attain'd,
By the dear swain that has her pity gain'd.

PERPLEXITY.

A POEM.

Ye tender young virgins attend to my lay,
  My heart is divided in twain;
My Collin is beautiful, witty, and gay,
  And Damon's a kind-hearted swain.

Whenever my lovely young Collin I meet,
  What pleasures arise in my breast;
The dear gentle swain looks so charming and sweet,
  I fancy I love him the best.

But when my dear Damon does to me complain,
  So tender, so loving and kind,
My bosom is soften'd to hear the fond swain,
  And Collin slips out of my mind.

Whenever my Damon repeats his soft tale,
  My heart overflows with delight;
But when my dear Collin appears in the vale,
  I languish away at the sight.

'Tis Collin alone shall possess my fond heart,
  Now Damon for ever adieu;
                                      But

But can I?—I cannot from Damon thus part!
  He's lov'd me so long, and so true.

My heart to my Damon I'll instantly bind,
  And on him will fix all my care;
But, O should I be to my Collin unkind,
  He surely will die with despair.

How happy, how happy with Damon I'd been,
  If Collin I never had knew;
As happy with Collin, if I'd never seen
  My Damon, so tender and true.

A PASTORAL SONG.

ONE ev'ning in May, the sweet season of love,
    Amintor, with heart light as air;
And his hat on one side, ran in haste to the grove,
    To meet his dear Delia there.

He waited a little, impatient no doubt,
    A minute to lovers is long;
Then snapping his fingers, he saunter'd about,
    And thus of his Delia sung.

My Delia is mild as an April morn,
    And fair as the blossoms in May
That sweeten the air, and enamel the thorn;
    She's fairer, she's sweeter than they!

So chearful and sprightly, good humour'd and gay,
    No passions e'er ruffle her breast;
In innocent frolicks she passes the day,
    Till ev'ning invites her to rest.

Let prudes and coquets to their artfulness trust,
    They ne'er shall have place in my arms;
Their wits and their arts do but give me disgust,
    'Tis virgin simplicity charms.

My lovely dear Delia's unſkill'd in their wiles,
   And all the coquetry of love:
She thoughtleſsly meets me, with innocent ſmiles,
   And trips with me into the grove.

Juſt then the fair Delia came tripping along,
   Diſplaying her innocent charms;
Amintor no longer continued his ſong,
   But claſp'd the dear maid in his arms.

The FAVOURITE SWAIN.

My generous muse, assistance lend;
Ye simple village-swains attend;
    I mean not to complain:
I'll tell you what the youth must be,
That hopes to gain the love of me,
    And be my Fav'rite Swain.

I ne'er can love the silly swain,
That quits the village and the plain,
    To flutter round the state;
Nor fool that leaves the woodbine bower,
To fix on that uncertain flower,
    The favour of the great:

But I some artless youth must find,
That knows not how to veil his mind,
    But speaks without disguise;
His count'nance cheering as the dawn,
That smiles upon the flowery lawn,
    And bids the sky-lark rise:

His eyes like dew-drops on the thorn,
When daisies opening to the morn,
                        Bespeak

Bespeak that morning fair;
His breath as sweet as western breeze,
That sweeps the sweetest smelling trees,
To scent the evening air.

And when he pipes upon the plain,
He must all approbation gain,
In spite of envious pride;
And force his rival swains to say,
His matchless skill must bear the sway,
It cannot be denied.

No passions like the northern wind,
Must discompose his steady mind,
By seriousness possest;
Yet sadness be as far away,
As darkest midnight from noon-day,
Or point of east from west.

His temper mild as April rain,
Whose gentle shower bedews the plain,
And gems the budding spray;
In manners like the lowly rill,
That creeps beneath the grassy hill,
Where shining fishes play.

No headstrong passion must incline
Him to my arms, or make him mine,
    But reason must approve;
To nicest honour be consign'd,
While virtue rules his generous mind,
    And friendship crowns his love.

Methinks the envious youths around,
Say such a one was never found,
    And all my search is vain:
Mistaken swains know this my song,
Does to my Thirsis all belong,
    For he's my Fav'rite Swain.

On a WEDDING.

Hark! hark! how the bells ring, how happy the day,
   Now Thirsis makes Daphne his bride;
See cheerful birds chirping on ev'ry green spray,
   And summer shines forth in its pride.

The lads and the lasses, so jocund and gay,
   Their happiness hail with a song;
And Thirsis enchantingly pipes to their lay,
   Inspiring with mirth all the throng.

The bride and the bride-groom then join in the dance
   And smiling trip nimbly around;
The sprightly gay bride's-maids as nimbly advance,
   And answer their smiles with a bound.

With all marriage articles pen'd on the heart,
   The parties so sweetly agreed;
They needed no lawyer, with quibbling art,
   Or parchment to draw up a deed.

For Love, the first blessing of blessings below,
   That Heaven to mortals can give,
Was all the kind shepherdess had to bestow,
   And all that she wish'd to receive.

LOB's COURTSHIP.

As Lob among his cows one day,
Was filling of their cribs with hay;
As he to th' crib the hay did carry,
It came into his head to marry;
Says he, there's little merry Nell,
I think I like her very well;
But she, perhaps, at me will scoff,
Besides, she lives a great way off:
He mus'd a while, then judg'd it better,
The courtship to begin by letter;
So he a bit of paper found,
'Twas neither long, nor square, nor round;
It was the best that he could find,
And on it thus, he wrote his mind:

Dear Nelly, I make bold to send
My love to you, and am your friend;
I think you are a pretty maid,
And wonder much that you don't wed;
If you can like a country man,
I'll come and see you, if I can,
When roads are good, and weather fine,
But first I hope you'll send a line.

Then he in haste this letter sent,

Also

Alſo two apples did preſent,
Which Nell receiv'd, and read the letter,
(But ſhe lik'd the apples better);
When read ſhe into the fire threw it,
And never ſent an anſwer to it.

When ſpring drew on, the cuckow ſung,
The roads were dry, and days were long,
The cows were all turn'd out to graſs,
Then Lob ſet out to ſee his laſs;
He oil'd his ſhoes, and comb'd his hair,
As if a going to a fair:
He was a very clever clown,
His frock was of the fuſtian brown,
His ſtick was bended like a bow,
His handkerchief too made a ſhow,
His hat ſtood like the pot-lid round,
So on he went, and Nell he found.

What Nelly! how doſt do? ſays he,
Come, will you go along with me
O'er yonder ſtile, a little way
Along that cloſe; Nell, what doſt ſay?

Me go with you o'er yonder ſtile?
Says Nell, indeed I can't a-while;
So ſhe ſtept in, and ſhut the door,
And he ſhabb'd off, and ſaid no more.

The RURAL MAID in LONDON,
To her FRIEND in the COUNTRY.

An EPISTLE.

REJOICE, dear nymph! enjoy your happy grove,
Where birds and shepherds warble strains of love,
While banish'd I, alas! can nothing hear,
But sounds too harsh to sooth a tender ear.
Here gilded beaux fine painted belles pursue,
But how unlike to village-swains and you;
At twelve o'clock they rub their slumb'ring eyes,
And, seeing day-light, from their pillows rise;
To the dear looking-glass due homage pay,
Look o'er the play-bills while they sip their tea;
Then order John the chariot to prepare,
And drive to th' Park, to take the morning air.
When dusky ev'ning spreads her gloomy shade,
And rural nymphs are in soft slumbers laid,
Then coaches rattle to the ladies rout,
With belles within, and mimic beaux without;
The vulgar way of counting time they scorn,
Their noon is evening, and their evening morn.

But

But what is yet more wonderful than all,
These strange disorders they do pleasures call:
Such tinsel joys shall ne'er my heart obtain,
Give me the real pleasures of the plain,
Where unmov'd constancy has fix'd her seat,
And love, and friendship, make their sweet retreat.
There lives my friend, my dear Belinda gay,
Could I with her the fresh'ning vales survey;
To make a wreath, I'd gather flow'rs full blown,
But spare the tender buds, till riper grown:
If I should see a black-bird, or a thrush,
Sit on her nest within the hawthorn bush,
She undisturb'd should hatch her little brood;
Who fright her thence has not a heart that's good;
It surely is a pity to molest,
A little bird, when sitting on her nest.
Should love by chance invite your friend to rove,
I'd take a trip into the silent grove;
There if my swain should pipe, then I would sing,
And be as happy as the birds in spring;
No title but a nymph I'd wish to know,
Nor e'er commence a belle, to win a beau.

CORINNA

CORINNA TO LYCIDAS.

WHERE'ER my Lycidas shall turn his eyes,
May pleasures spring, and lovely prospects 'rise;
While your Corinna, on the banks of Stower,
In pensive sadness views each ripening flower:
Why am I pensive? all things else are gay,
Fawns dance around, and harmless lambkins play;
Surrounding groves invite my steps to rove,
Resembling that in which I learn'd to love;
They each returning morn, grow fresher still,
And happy birds their leafy branches fill;
O lovely scenes! but what are these to me?
Joy is no joy without society.
If I a friend like Lycidas could find,
To share my joys, or sooth my anxious mind;
Then morn and night, I'd tune my cheerful lay,
Sing with the birds, and be more glad than they;
But while your absence I am doom'd to bear,
Your fancied presence in my thoughts shall share;
I'll bless the hour in which our love began,
And ever be as constant as I can.

An EPISTLE.

My dear Maria, my long abſent friend,
If you can ſpare one moment to attend,
The plaintive ſtrains of your Belinda hear,
Who is your friend, and as yourſelf ſincere.
Let love-ſick nymphs their faithful ſhepherds prove,
Maria's friendſhip's more to me than love;
When you were here, I ſmil'd throughout the day,
No ruſtic ſhepherdeſs was half ſo gay;
But now, alas! I can no pleaſure know,
The tedious hours of abſence move ſo ſlow;
I ſecret mourn, not daring to complain,
Still ſeeking for relief, but ſeek in vain.

When I walk forth to take the morning air,
I quickly to ſome riſing hill repair,
From whence I may ſurvey your village ſpire,
Then ſigh to you, and languiſh with deſire.

At ſultry noon retiring to the groves,
In ſearch of you, my wand'ring fancy roves,
From ſhade to ſhade, pleas'd with the vain delight,
Imagination brings you to my ſight;

Fatigu'd

Fatigu'd I sink into my painted chair,
And your ideal form attends me there.

My garden claims one solitary hour,
When sober ev'ning closes ev'ry flow'r;
The drooping lily my resemblance bears,
Each pensive bloom a shining dew-drop wears;
Such shining drops my closing eyes bedew,
While I am absent from the sight of you.

When on my couch reclin'd my eyes I close,
The God of Sleep refuses me repose;
I 'rise half dress'd, and wander to and fro
Along my room, or to my window go:
Enraptur'd I behold the moon shine clear,
While falling waters murmur in my ear;
My thoughts to you then in a moment fly,
The moon shines misty, and my raptures die.

Thus ev'ry scene a gloomy prospect wears,
And ev'ry object prompts Belinda's tears:
'Tis you, Maria, and 'tis only you,
That can the wonted face of things renew:
Come to my groves; command the birds to sing,
And o'er the meadows bid fresh daisies spring:
No! rather come and chase my gloom away,
That I may sing like birds, and look like daisies gay.

LEANDER

LEANDER AND BELINDA.

A TALE.

BELINDA is the lovelieſt fair,
  Of all the rural train,
That dance upon the flow'ry lawn,
  Or trip acroſs the plain.

Her pleaſing air, and winning grace,
  The village ſwains admire;
But not a youth in all that place,
  To court her durſt aſpire.

Her robes were of the whiteſt lawn,
  As ſpotleſs as her fame;
And all the bluſhing virgin train,
  Rever'd Belinda's name.

At laſt her fame Leander hears,
  Who in the city dwells;
And he, for this fair village-maid,
  Forſook the city belles.

His

His coat was of the crimson dye,
    His spurs were silver bright;
And thus equip'd away he rode,
    To court this nymph in white.

With each acquir'd accomplishment
    Endow'd, and on his tongue
The pow'rful art of flattery,
    In full persuasion hung.

He told to her such pleasing tales,
    As anxious lovers tell;
Such as he'd often told before,
    To many a shining belle.

Into the garden walk'd this pair,
    To view the flowers gay;
Belinda look'd like lilies fair,
    That grew about the way.

By her fair hand Leander took,
    This lovely charming maid;
Like Strephon's flocks at summer's noon,
    From shade to shade they stray'd.

They walk'd 'till drooping dewy flow'rs,
    Proclaim'd the ev'ning nigh;
And that sweet bird that sings i' th' air,
    Descended from the sky.   Lean-

Leander seeing nature's pride,
  The tales of ev'ning tell,
He with reluctancy retir'd,
  And bade his nymph farewell.

But vow'd he quickly would return,
  And make the fair one his;
Then with an oath his promise bound,
  And seal'd it with a kiss.

Yet the next news Belinda hears,
  Is that Leander's wed;
A wealthier, not a fairer dame,
  He to the church had led.

But ere the honey-moon was past,
  A fever seiz'd his bride;
And though he left nor pains, nor cost,
  Nor medicine untry'd.

Not all the skill'd physician's art,
  Could heal his sicken'd spouse;
Cosmelia died, a just reward
  For all his broken vows.

OBSERVA-

OBSERVATION,

On an EVENING.

Sweet and refreshing are the dews,
  That deck the ev'ning shade;
Sweet are the winds that sweep the plains,
  And whisper through the glade.

We faint beneath the sultry sun,
  But when the day is o'er,
We gladly meet the ev'ning shade,
  And think of toil no more.

REFLECTION.

So when the dew of heav'nly grace,
  Falls gently on the soul,
It cheers the fainting, drooping heart,
  And bids new pleasures roll:

To ev'ry doubt, and ev'ry fear,
  This brings a sweet relief;
Superior joy! compar'd with this,
  All other joy is grief.

Written

Written while the AUTHOR sat on a COCK of HAY.

FAIR Daphne to the meadow went,
  To tedd the new mown hay;
    She went alone,
    For well 'twas known,
  No shepherd went that way.

And when she to the meadow came,
  And cast her eyes around,
    She saw green hills,
    And purling rills,
  The fertile spot surround.

The alders and the poplars tall,
  Did form a circling shade;
    The cooling breeze,
    Stole by the trees,
  Along the open glade.

Beneath the shade a murm'ring brook,
  Pursues its crooked way;

There fishes glide,
In conscious pride,
And shining scales display.

The beauteous blooming gifts of spring,
Are fallen from the thorn;
But the wild rose,
More beauteous grows,
The willow tree t' adorn.

The sun that o'er Arabian fields,
Bids spicy odours play;
By the same pow'r,
Doth in an hour,
Raise sweetness from the hay.

The choristers from ev'ry grove,
In num'rous bands appear;
From spray to spray,
Tune forth their lay,
To charm the virgin's ear.

But yet amidst this pleasing scene,
Our nymph doth sullen prove;
Such things says she,
Might pleasure me,
If I was not in love.

To cheerful ſtrains I'll not aſpire,
　　Since fate that led me here,
　　　　Forbids my ſwain,
　　　　To tread this plain,
　　I'll drop a ſilent tear.

On CONTEMPLATIVE EASE.

Rejoice ye jovial sons of mirth,
   By sparkling wine inspir'd;
A joy of more intrinsic worth
   I feel, while thus retir'd.

Excluded from the ranting crew,
   Amongst these fragrant trees
I walk, the twinkling stars to view,
   In solitary ease.

Half wrap'd in clouds, the half-form'd moon
   Beams forth a cheering ray,
Surpassing all the pride of noon,
   Or charms of early day.

The birds are hush'd, and not a breeze
   Disturbs the pendant leaves;
My passion's hush'd as calm as these,
   No sigh my bosom heaves.

While great ones make a splendid show,
   In equipage or dress,
I'm happy here, nor wish below
   For greater happiness.

Written

Written on Their MAJESTIES coming to KEW.

HE comes, he comes, our sacred King,
  Now bids the town adieu;
And all the bells at Richmond ring,
  To welcome him to Kew.

The air serene, the ev'ning clear,
  The moon so fair to view;
Sweet emblem of our gracious Queen,
  That came to day to Kew.

Now softly blows the western gale,
  To waft the joyful strains,
Along the lowly winding vale,
  And tell the distant plains.

In Spring's fresh robes the trees are clad,
  The fields are fair to view;
And every loyal heart is glad
  The King is come to Kew.

Ye lovers of inconstancy,
  Now blush and take a view;

A bright example you may see,
  The royal pair at Kew.

May God continue still to give
  Them pleasures ever new;
And many summers may they live
  To reign and visit Kew.

CONTENTMENT.

WHILST I beneath this silent shade,
  Contented sit and sing,
I envy not the great their joys,
  That from their riches spring.

Let those who have in courts been bred,
  There still in splendor shine;
Their lot of bliss may not surpass,
  Perhaps not equal mine,

While no unwelcome visitants,
  My solitude invade;
The monarch is not more secure,
  Than I beneath this shade.

These friendly trees on either side,
  From heat a shelter stand;
The white rose on the brier hangs,
  And seems t' invite my hand.

Ah! rose, no longer to my eyes
  Thy pow'rful charms display,
For I've a sweeter flow'r than you,
  And one that looks more gay.

The WIDOWER's COURTSHIP.

Roger a doleful widower,
  Full eighteen weeks had been,
When he, to meet the milk-maid Nell,
  Came ſmiling o'er the green.

Blithe as a lad of ſeventeen,
  He thus accoſted Nell;
Give me your pail, I'll carry it
  For you, if you think well.

Says Nell, indeed my milking-pail
  You ſhall not touch, I vow;
I've carried it myſelf before,
  And I can carry it now.

So ſide by ſide they walk'd a-while,
  Then he at laſt did ſay;
My inclination is to come
  And ſee you, if I may.

Nell underſtood his meaning well,
  And briſkly anſwer'd ſhe;
You may ſee me at any time,
  If you look where I be.   Says

Says he, but hear me yet a-while,
  I've something more to tell;
I gladly wou'd a sweetheart be
  Unto you, Miſtreſs Nell.

A sweetheart I don't want, ſays Nell,
  Kind Sir, and if you do,
Another you may ſeek, for I
  Am not the laſs for you.

When ſhe had made him this reply,
  He'd nothing more to ſay
But—Nelly, a good night to you,
  And homeward went his way.

OBSERVATION
ON THE
WORKS of NATURE.

Now night submits to the encroaching day,
And groves, and fields, put on their spring array;
Now various flowers of various hues display'd,
Adorn the green, or deck the lonely shade.
These show the pow'r of the Almighty's hand;
They spring, they blow, they fade at his command:
United Nature does his word fulfil,
'Tis Man alone rejects his Maker's will.

An ELEGY.

OH where, Oh where are all those joys,
That in ten thousand forms arise,
   T' elude the wand'ring eye,
When youth its vigorous charms displays,
And beauty sheds its softening rays
   To move the wishful sigh.

Ah! youth is but a summer's morn,
When shining drops the fields adorn,
   Their twinkling soon is o'er:
So beauty by encroaching years
Exhilarates and disappears,
   And youth returns no more.

What happiness attends the pair,
Whose bliss no low intruding care,
   Or adverse fates destroy;
When youth and beauty disappears,
Their virtues, ripening with their years,
   Increase their mutual joy.

But how, Oh! how can I relate
The heart-felt tale—the hapless fate?

Where are you gone, my tears?
O come and give my heart relief,
For Collin's dead, alas! and grief
   Embitters Hebe's years.

When health fat blooming on his face,
And beauty with resplendent grace,
   In every feature shone;
Voracious death seiz'd on his prey,
No warning sickness mark'd his way;
   He died—alas, he's gone!

When rosy health, with flattering smiles,
Th' unwary thoughtless youth beguiles,
   He counts his coming years;
Presumptuous man! by Collin's fate,
Learn to contract the doubtful date,
   And pity Hebe's tears.

FRIEND-

FRIENDSHIP.

An ODE.

Friendship infpires;
The facred lay
My bofom fires;
Let friendly virgins tune their lyres,
In concert join, angelic choirs,
    Due rites to pay.

Let envy fhrink away,
As darknefs flies approaching day;
Her ferpent creft in vain fhe rears,
    And her curft fting prepares;
She counteracts herfelf; for fee
    Her blaft,
    Binds faft
The knot of friendfhip ty'd,
    In virtuous pride,
    And firm fincerity.

O friendfhip, firft of bleffings here below,
  The beft gift Heaven can beftow!

Thou secret balm,
Serene and calm;
O stream of bliss, in gentlest currents flow!

Calm, humble bliss of friendship rise,
Superior to the splendid joys,
That glitter round the world;
Temptations so profusely spread,
With dazzling glares mislead
The feet that heedless tread,
And all those joys are in confusion hurl'd.

But Oh! 'tis friendship's rite,
To give and take delight,
Dividing care:
Fly hence, despair,
Nor more annoy;
Firm friendship's joy
Shines undiminish'd in distress,
The wretched and the blest to bless;
Its sweet and sovereign power let every tongue
confess.

PHILLIS

PHILLIS TO DAMON.

A SONG.

REmember, false Damon, how often you've said,
You lov'd me as well as a man could a maid;
Though you slight me at last, and I cannot tell why,
Yet, trust me, I never with sorrow shall die.

In my bosom so tender, your power to prove,
You planted the fair blooming flow'ret of love;
But for its destruction a frown you prepar'd,
To blast at your pleasure the flowret you rear'd.

Yet boast not your conquest, tho' from me you part,
Nor think yourself wholly possess'd of my heart;
Your smiles are not summer to melt the cold snow,
And your frowns are not winter, I'd have you to know.

Go seek for a maid that has money in store,
And amuse yourself often in counting it o'er;
Yet, Damon, believe me, your bliss will be small,
If counting your gold and your silver be all.

He that sets his heart riches and honour to find,
Will learn that a kingdom's too small for his mind;
He hoards up his treasures, and thinks himself scant,
While the poor that's contented ne'er feels any want.

The joys of the wealthy are joys of a day,
For riches have wings and do oft fly away;
And when they are flying we generally find,
A long train of sorrow's impending behind.

May all pleasures attend you, that treasures can bring,
May you find of your joys a perpetual spring;
Yet I'll envy her not, that has money in store,
Nor think myself wretched, although I am poor.

Perhaps I the truth of some shepherd may prove,
Whose treasure's contentment, whose pleasure is love;
Then I without wealth shall be happy as you,
So Damon, false Damon, for ever adieu.

On an UNSOCIABLE FAMILY.

O What a strange parcel of creatures are we,
Scarce ever to quarrel, or ever agree;
We all are alone, though at home altogether,
Except to the fire constrain'd by the weather;
Then one says, 'tis cold, which we all of us know,
And with unanimity answer, 'tis so:
With shrugs and with shivers all look at the fire,
And shuffle ourselves and our chairs a bit nigher;
Then quickly, preceded by silence profound,
A yawn epidemical catches around:
Like social companions we never fall out,
Nor ever care what one another's about;
To comfort each other is never our plan,
For to please ourselves, truly, is more than we can.

REFLECTION on MEDITATION.

TO earth it bows the knees, but lifts the soul
So high above all sublunary things,
That this low world shews like a fleeting dream
Already past away.

On reading Pope's Eloiza *to* Abelard.

SURE, haplefs Fair, no hearts can ever know,
But banifh'd lovers, banifh'd lovers' woe!
Ah! Eloiza, ever exil'd maid,
I read thy forrows, forrowing as I read:
My fympathetic heart now fhares thy grief,
Repeats thy fighs, and wifhes thy relief:
But when I hear thee unrelenting boaft
Thy tainted virtue, and thy honour loft,
All fenfe of pity in my bofom dies,
And direful tumults of reproaches rife:
No paffions foft, or fadly-pleafing pain,
But rage and madnefs in thy bofom reign;
Ah! muft thy Abelard exalted be,
Above the Maker of himfelf and thee!
And dareft thou thus explode the wedded dame,
Difclaim her virtues, and difdain her fame:
Blufh, Eloiza, at a thought fo vain,
Thy face with crimfon let confufion ftain;
And while thy bofom glows with guilty fire,
Let every hope of happinefs expire;
But if again thou would'ft my pity move,
Lament at once thy honour and thy love.
Written,

Written, originally extempore, on seeing a MAD HEIFER *run through the* VILLAGE *where the* AUTHOR *lives.*

WHEN summer smil'd, and birds on ev'ry spray,
In joyous warblings tun'd their vocal lay,
Nature on all sides shew'd a lovely scene,
And people's minds were, like the air, serene;
Sudden from th' herd we saw an heifer stray,
And to our peaceful village bend her way.
She spurns the ground with madness as she flies,
And clouds of dust, like autumn mists, arise;
Then bellows loud: the villagers alarm'd,
Come rushing forth, with various weapons arm'd:
Some run with pieces of old broken rakes,
And some from hedges pluck the rotten stakes;
Here one in haste, with hand-staff of his flail,
And there another comes with half a rail:
Whips, without lashes, sturdy plough-boys bring,
While clods of dirt and pebbles others fling:
Voices tumultuous rend the listening ear;
Stop her—one cries; another—turn her there:
But furiously she rushes by them all,
And some huzza, and some to cursing fall:

A mo-

A mother snatch'd her infant off the road,
Close to the spot of ground where next she trod;
Camilla walking, trembled and turn'd pale;
See o'er her gentle heart what fears prevail!
At last the beast, unable to withstand
Such force united, leapt into a pond:
The water quickly cool'd her madden'd rage;
No more she'll fright our village, I presage.

A SONG.

A SONG.

YE swains cease to flatter, our hearts to obtain,
If your persons plead not, what your tongues say
    is vain;
Though fickle you call us, believe me you're wrong,
We're fixt as a rock, as a rock too are strong.

Though sometimes, when suddenly struck with
    your charms,
We melt into softness, and sink in your arms,
Or breathe a soft sigh, when you from us depart;
That shakes not the purpose that's firm in the heart.

Too vainly ye boast we are easily won;
If on you, as on all, we should smile like the sun,
You laugh in your sleeves, when you from us retire,
And think that we love, when we only admire.

We are not so easily led by the nose,
Though with coxcombs we chatter, and flirt with
    the beaux;
Yet seldom or never our hearts they command,
Though sometimes through pity we give them our
    hand.

A tony, a coxcomb, a beau, or a clown,
Well feafon'd with money, may fometimes go down;
But thefe in our hearts we can never revere;
The worthy man only can hold a place there.

A SONG.

FAR from the woods, alas, I rove,
Far from the fwain I dearly love:
Sure fome ill ftar did rule the day,
When firft my heedlefs feet did ftray,
From my dear fwain fo far away.

'Tis now the morning of the fpring,
And larks and linnets fweetly fing;
I might have fung as well as they,
If I had never learnt to ftray,
From my dear fwain fo far away.

Oh! that I had ne'er left the plain,
Oh! that I could return again;
But here I mourn my abject ftate,
Like a poor dove that's loft her mate,
And figh, alas! but figh too late.

A SONG.

A SONG.

WHEN Chloe, smiling, gave consent,
  To be Philander's bride,
Name but the time, and I'm content,
  Th' enraptur'd shepherd cry'd.

Next Sunday morn, says Doris soon,
  Shall be the happy hour;
And I, with all the flow'rs of June,
  Will deck the nuptial bow'r.

But Doris counteracts the plan,
  How sly the artful maid;
She smil'd, and won the am'rous man,
  And Chloe was betray'd.

With joy the swain produc'd the ring,
  For Chloe once design'd;
And Doris, cheerful as the spring,
  Was to Philander join'd.

No nuptial bow'r on Sunday morn,
  For Chloe deck'd shall be;
The slighted maid may sigh forlorn,
  Beneath the willow tree.

ABSENCE.

When Collin's tuneful pipe with soft'ning strains,
Fill'd with melodious sounds the neighb'ring plains;
The nightingale responsive, in the grove
Sung her sweet lay, and tun'd my heart to love:
But absent now from all that's to me dear,
A charm in Music I no longer hear.

Where are the joys the early seasons bring?
For herds the grass, for bees the flowers spring;
The black-birds sing on ev'ry blooming thorn,
And fresh'ning daisies ev'ry vale adorn:
In vain the spring for me adorns the plains,
While in my heart so cold a winter reigns.

The herds in Summer seek the cooling streams,
Where shady trees exclude the sultry beams;
The shepherds to some op'ning glade repair,
Where gentle breezes temperate the air:
But no cool breeze can fan my flame away,
Nor cooler streams the latent fire allay.

Rich Autumn now adds profit to delight,
And rip'ning apples ev'ry hand invite;

Each

Each swain divides his apple with his fair,
So I with Collin once was wont to share:
But now no fruits to please my taste have pow'r,
Not gather'd by his hand, all fruits are sour.

Winter a-while each growing herb restrains,
And locks all nature in his icy chains;
His reign but for a season doth endure,
Spring smiles, and nature feels the pow'rful cure:
But ah! my heart's in faster fetters bound,
Which still grow stronger as the years go round.

To THIRSIS,

On his signifying his intention to lay aside his HAUTBOY.

What spurious offspring of low-thoughted care
Assumes the graceful muses winning air,
And bids my Thirsis lay aside his reed,
That dulness may serenity succeed;
This step still onward her dark purpose brings,
For out of dulness, melancholy springs;
Nor here the gloomy phantom ends her care,
For next to melancholy, comes despair:
When fainting virtue makes her slow retreat,
Vice ready stands, to fill the vacant seat.
Oft have I seen the swains assembled round,
With silent awe, till Thirsis led the sound:
Still, as your breath, the cheering pipe inspires,
Conduct the voices of the hymning choirs:
If thou, their leader and support should'st fail,
Slack negligence will o'er the rest prevail;
No more the evenings of the holy-days,
Shall send to Heav'n their well-accepted lays;
But giddy youths to vanities shall run,
Nay, well if darker scenes of vice they shun.

On the Author's LYING-IN,

AUGUST, 1785.

O God, the giver of all joy,
Whose gifts no mortal can destroy,
 Accept my grateful lays:
My tongue did almost ask for death,
But thou did'st spare my lab'ring breath,
 To sing thy future praise.

I live! my God be prais'd, I live,
And do most thankfully receive,
 The bounty of my life:
I live, still longer to improve,
The fondest husband's tender love,
 To the most happy wife.

I live within my arms to clasp,
My infant with endearing grasp,
 And feel my fondness grow:
O God endow her with thy grace,
And heav'nly gifts, to hold a place
 Among thy Saints below.

May

May she in duty, as she ought,
By thy unerring precepts taught,
   To us a blessing prove:
And thus prepar'd for greater joys,
May she, with thine elect arise
   To taste the joys above.

An ENIGMA.

I Come, a friend to man, I'm ne'er his foe
But when he indiscreetly makes me so.
My name is——Stop tho'—what am I about?
They that would know my name may find it out.

I'm seen in Summer in the shady grove,
Where pensive speculating maidens rove;
And when the verdure of the forest flies
Before th' Autumnal winds, that blust'ring rise
To waft the yellow fragments o'er the plain,
Firm and unshaken still my leaves remain;
But in the Winter I some covert crave,
Nor dare the rigour of that season brave:
Yet if too near the fire I take my stand,
My rind contracts, and leaves too much expand;
Doctors extract my essence and apply't
To stop disorders, and to give delight;
And some that would my properties define,
Declare I am essentially divine:
Nay some, by arrant superstition taught,
Say I immediately from Heav'n was brought;
But that I am in Heav'n, let none deny,
The Scripture says it, can the Scripture lye?

CRI-

CRITICAL FRAGMENTS,

ON SOME OF THE
ENGLISH POETS.

MILTON, in pond'rous verse, moves greatly on,
Weilding his massy theme; with wond'rous strength
He labours forward.

   SHAKESPEAR gently glides,
And, like a polish'd mirror, as he passes
Reflects all nature.

   YOUNG, in thought profound,
Muses, contemplates, sees, and feels the woes
That clog the soul; yet with aspiring wing
Behold him 'rise majestically flow,
And like an eagle soar, and soar aloft:

  But SWIFT delights as much to rout
  I'th' dirt, and then to throw't about.

POPE sings a soft and sweet harmonious lay,
So mellow flutes in pleasant concert play.

MATT.

MATT. PRIOR, like an eafy horfe,
Keeps ambling on, ne'er out of courfe:

But trotting BUTLER beats him hollow,
He leads a way that none can follow;
He dafhes on through thick and thin,
Nor for the criticks cares a pin;
From cenfure he's receiv'd acquittal,
And grammar, metre, rhyme fubmit all.

F I N I S.

ERRATA.

Page 4, line 13, for *Shimlah,* read *Shimeah.*—Page 4, line 18, for *its,* read *his.*—Page 12, line 1, for *Amnon's,* read *Ammon's.*—Page 19, line 15, for *To my inexperienced,* read *My inexperienced.*—Page 20, line 7, add a Note of Interrogation after *young man?*—Page 27, line 14, for *fhall,* read *fhalt.*

www.ingramcontent.com/pod-product-compliance
Lightning Source LLC
Chambersburg PA
CBHW020312170426
43202CB00008B/579